CONTENT
SUCCESS STOI

➜   Read these and know that the possibilities
for your projects are endless!

"One phone call with Squeaky Moore and I went from a bit directionless and somewhat passive to inspired, encouraged – re-energized in the pursuit of my dreams.

Her passion is infectious; her enthusiasm is sincere. Squeaky truly believes in the independent creator (being one herself), and deeply desires for each and every one of us who travels this uncertain road to achieve success.

But it's not all rah-rah. After briefly sketching out my project, Squeaky saw right to the heart of the issues and began suggesting strategies – nuts and bolts, step-by-step actions that I could take to move forward. As valuable as her unflagging encouragement was, to have her propose a plan with achievable goals, tailored to the specifics of my project – this was the most meaningful aspect of her consultation.

If you have a desire to move your project closer to success and a willingness to take the steps necessary to realize that progress, then by all means contact Squeaky. She will immediately become an enthusiastic advocate for your project; and with her hard-won, real-world experience, she will quickly come up with pragmatic advice and an actionable plan for your success.

Getting Squeaky Moore on your team could be the wisest thing you do for the future of your project!"

—John E. Ellis

"While researching to present my pitch to producers I came across Squeaky's webinar on her Nine Rules of Pitching. (There were probably more but I really only remembered nine.) It was a real eye-opener and gave practical concrete steps to be as prepared as possible before stepping foot in the room. A lifesaver for anyone about to take a meeting with potential collaborators. She gives you straight up advice and doesn't sugar coat it. I got my current deal using her techniques and can honestly say that if you follow her rules, you'll probably walk out with a deal."

—Greg Paul

"I got in my own way! But Squeaky helped me break out of a holding pattern and helped me to develop and finalize a fantastic pitch. I knew I could trust her judgment and her expertise to guide me in creating the perfect pitch. I now have the tools to pitch effectively every time. She took the time to connect with me in an authentic way. She quickly identified ways to make my pitch more effective in order to reach my specific demographic of women. She helped me create universal themes from my story that could reach a broader audience. Squeaky encouraged me in a way that built my confidence, shared lots of tips, and gave examples of written and verbal pitches. She took the time to hear my story and understand my perspective, gave me homework, and encouraged me along the way. She helped me identify themes that were not ready for pitching and directed me to work on the other areas that had more potential. She empowered me by giving me the tools to 'do my own work'; now I can use what she taught me to pitch other ideas and products."

—Alicia Moss, Entrepreneur, Educator & Exhorter
www.MossGirls.com

#100PITCHES

MISTAKES I'VE MADE SO YOU DON'T HAVE TO

BY SQUEAKY MOORE

The Film and Television Pitching Guide
for Independent Content Creators

MOORE
SQUEAKY PRODUCTIONS

For information about special discounts for bulk purchases, please contact Moore Squeaky Productions at support@thepitch101.com.

To bring Squeaky Moore to your live event or for more information about speaking engagements, panels, and workshops, please contact Moore Squeaky Productions at info@thepitch101.com.

Cover design by Gerald Yarborough
Editing by Stacie Nielsen Bortel, www.Nielsenbortel.com

ISBN-13: 978-0692898451
ISBN-10: 069289845X
Moore Squeaky Productions
www.squeakymoore.com

DEDICATION

This book is dedicated to my biggest support system, my family. Will, my supportive and loving husband, you have held down the fort and been my biggest fan. I am forever grateful for your loving kindness and your great friendship. Thank you for being everything I could ask for in a husband. I am truly blessed. Michai, my helpmate, you are always in tune with me and I thank you for hanging by my side quietly as I write. You get me. Cree, thanks for being my spirited warrior. You put the fire beneath me. Thank you all for supporting me and patiently sharing me with the world. I appreciate you greatly!

To my mom, dad, and my sister Nanette, while you rest in heaven I feel your love, hugs, and nudges of support. This book is in loving memory of you. You are the wind beneath my wings.

To my loving sisters and brothers, Rhontese, Sheresa, LaShaun, Nookie, Lydell, and Lionel, I love you all deeply. To my two nieces, Ashlee and Krissy – who keep me in the loop – thanks for your group texts and edits. Lol.

To my in-laws, God gave you to me. Mom and dad, thanks for including me in your family like I was your own. Thanks for taking care of me and mine while I become great. It is "us against the world." Tee Tee, thanks for holding down the fort. There is no way I could have written this book without you.

To my sounding board, mastermind, and accountability friends, "The Bold and The Beautiful," Kristen L. Pope, and Joresa Blount, you have watched me closely on this journey and have pushed me every step of the way. What on earth would I do without your daily motivation? You help me move the needle.

Last, to all of you who walked with me on this journey, I can't thank you enough. Heather-Sky – it is because of you that this book even exists! To my marketing and branding mentors, Tatiana Holifield and Sybil Amuti, thanks for letting me pick your brains. Those few hours of your marketing and branding genius were priceless. Danielle Wright, I appreciate you for believing in me and sending me periodic inspirational messages. You allowed me to brainstorm my thoughts about public relations and listened patiently on the other end of the phone, then took my ideas and ran with them. I'm truly grateful for your time. Gerald Yarborough, you are the best graphic designer ever! Thanks for seeing my concepts through and adding your expertise. Lastly, I sincerely appreciate all of the experts that poured into me and every one who reads this book. Thanks for lending your expertise.

My Mission

Helping the independent content creator,

especially minorities and women,

get their stories heard one pitch at a time.

CONTENTS

LET'S STAY CONNECTED

The Pitch 101 Community

The pitch 101 community is a resource to help the independent content creator bridge the gap between independent and mainstream. It's a community of likeminded filmmakers, directors, writers and producers who commune to give tips, encouragement, and support to each other. It's a place where we all can connect and celebrate each other's successes, big and small. It's where I extend more help to those of you who are seeking to create and pitch ideas in a masterful way.

Every day, the positive, ambitious, and supportive people who are in this group blow me away. I honestly had no idea when I created this forum that the environment would be filled with such positivity and creativity.

I want to stay connected with you. Just go to ThePitch101Community and ask to join The Pitch 101 Community on Facebook. I would love to have you join us.

I am the host of the group and am always checking in regularly. I look forward to seeing you there!

If you want to connect with me personally, here are some other ways to do that:

Subscribe to my blog, The Pitch 101: http://www.thepitch101.com
Twitter: @squeakymoore
My personal Facebook page: @squeakymoore

A NOTE TO THE READER

To those of you who desire to tell your stories to the world by any means necessary

Pitching is an art form! Pitching takes almost as much creativity as it does to create a film or television show and write it. The single most important thing one can do before pitching, is prepare. You know what they say, "preparation meets opportunity." Well, preparation is everything to a pitch! You can't go wrong if you've prepared well, because if you've prepared well, it's in your heart; your story, your characters, your passion, and your world are all in your heart. It's your story, for you to tell it like it is.

JUST START WITH THE STORY!

PREFACE

Pitch #1: And so the Journey Begins

Every dream is captured twice;
first in the mental, then in the physical.
—Mark Batterson

It's August 26th, 2015, and I'm headed to 36th and Broadway to meet Tracey Baker-Simmons, Executive Producer of *Being Bobby Brown* and *The Houston's*, to pitch. When she said to meet her on 36th street, I didn't know I'd be pitching her my show ideas outside in New York City's busy streets. I had prepared to pitch two different show concepts, but after taking in the unexpected surroundings, I decided to only pitch one idea.

The producer, a woman I invited a couple of years before to my premiere party for a short film I'd produced, (that she didn't attend), was available to meet with me on this day. I'd spent the prior year building a relationship with her on social media and finally asked her for an informational interview to get her advice on working in development, [a person that searches for material to be turned into films of television shows], since she had been a development executive at a production company. We met at Michael Jordan's Steakhouse for a cocktail to "discuss the challenges of development."

I was nervous as hell, to say the least. But, I had practiced my pitch several times already, including on the walk over from the Viacom offices where I worked at the time. In my bag was my PowerPoint deck that I would use to pitch my show. I had spent a few weeks developing the concept: I was ready. My show was a reality format competition show. This producer would be the perfect person to help me because of her previous work with music artists, including executive producing a successful reality series with some amazing music artists.

As I was pitching her, I sensed that she was excited about my show idea. She was reserved, don't get me wrong, but *what* she said indicated how she felt about my project. Statements like, *"We'd probably want to reach out to production companies internationally, first. I suggest you hold off on pitching until you've created a format bible and registered it with the Writers Guild of America"* hinted that I was up to something good.

She asked, "Do you know how to do a format bible?"

"Yes, I'm familiar with them," I responded.

I lied. I didn't know how to do a format bible. But when she suggested I do one, I figured it couldn't be much harder than creating a pitch bible. I had created a pitch bible for a drama series before, but I soon realized that though they had similarities, they were also very different.

A pitch bible is a sales tool that helps to communicate your story concept. It is used to fully create the world of your show and it's character's. It is also used to help the buyer understand your concept as you see it. While there aren't any cookie cutter rules to what goes in it and how it should be designed, there are basic elements that shouldn't be left out.

I left the meeting excited. Speaking with her gave me hope for my show. I rushed back to work. I wanted to get started on the bible right away. Time was of the essence. I copied all the information from my pitch deck into a Word document, and then started wondering what else could possibly go into the format bible. All of a sudden, the word *format* frightened me. At a loss, I decided to reach out to her and ask for her help. I wanted to ask her in a way that seemed like I hadn't lied to her earlier. I asked, "Do you have any samples or templates of a format bible?" I told her I didn't want to leave anything out that she specifically thought should be included, and I wanted to make sure it was in a format she preferred. Looking back, it was such a dumb lie. But, I was following the *fake it till you make it* rule. Luckily, she sent me a format bible checklist without commenting on my lie.

I was so overwhelmed with creating the format bible! There were so many bullets on the checklist that I had never thought of. I had sufficiently developed my show idea, or so I thought. In my mind, copying all of the information from my pitch deck would make completing the bible easy-breezy. It was much more complicated than that. I had never thought through much of the information I needed to include, and I really didn't have a clue what some items were referring to.

Two months passed and I still hadn't completed the proposal. There were several items on the checklist, like preparing an executive summary that halted me. For the first time, I understood that to be creative and get my show on air meant that I also had to understand the business of formats in every sense. I had to be more than creative; I had to be a businesswoman.

· According to Wikipedia, a TV format is the overall concept and branding of a copyrighted television programming, like in reality shows or game shows.

As I completed the bible, I realized I hadn't thought through the world of my show to the smallest detail. While I had a great concept, I hadn't visualized it moment for moment, meaning the element, the style, the mood, the colors, or its design. There were many visual elements missing. The question I hadn't thought to ask myself was, *"What will people see when they sit on their sofas and watch my hour-long show?"* In truth, it felt like I was starting all over from the beginning, and the thought of doing more work on a concept I thought I had completed was overwhelming. Yet, I was excited to learn more about properly developing my ideas so I could be better prepared to pitch. More importantly, I realized that reaching out to executives to pitch my show before creating a format bible was making me look like a novice, and I was probably sending all kinds of red flags to the professionals. I had to cease all forms of pitching until I knew the workings of my show inside and out, and the only way to do that was to complete the format bible.

There were still a couple of items on the checklist I was unsure about. I wasn't familiar with some of the terminology used in the checklist and until then, I had never heard of the content creator doing an executive summary for their show. It's my truth. This is how green I was to the business side of pitching.

I asked several content creators in my immediate network for help, but I learned nothing more than what I knew before. I'd even asked a friend to ask her boss, who was a vice president in development at a network, if she knew what the checklist was asking me to do. To my surprise, the development executive didn't know either; she had never seen or heard of this "checklist" for the format bible.

I was stuck. I now understood that unless the network produced competition shows, they were just as clueless as I was. It makes sense to me now, but it didn't before then.

I was left with one single option: to return to the producer with my tail between my legs and ask her how to do an executive summary for my shows. I felt embarrassed that I didn't know this stuff. I didn't want her to know that I had never done an executive summary. As a content creator, I'm very proud. I was afraid she would decide not to work with me based on my lack of knowledge.

What would you think of me if I said I didn't ask her? Would you have asked? Well, I did – albeit two months later, but I asked. If I didn't feel it would help so many content creators to know my truth and share the lesson I learned from waiting to ask the necessary questions to complete the task, I promise I would have left it out. But, you deserve the truth. Many of you reading this are just like me, too afraid to ask the essential questions you need to in order to progress in your career. If you are like me, it's because you don't want to appear ignorant or like a novice, so you say nothing. You continue to *fake it til' you make it.*

I kept telling myself, *"There are no dumb questions. All questions are good questions."* I went back to the executive producer and asked if she had any executive summary templates for television shows. What I was hoping to learn was how to do an executive summary for the show that I was creating. She said she would check to see, but to no avail. I was left in limbo, so I decided to set up our next meeting with what I had, which was my format bible, sans the executive summary.

It was this experience that made me want to write this book. I wondered how many others out there were like me. It bothered me that I couldn't find the information on the Internet. I have found a lot of it after I set out on this journey, but the problem was I didn't know what I was looking for. I didn't know the lingo to do a proper search, and it was mixed amongst so many different articles and books that I would have had to either be in the know or a great researcher to find it all. I came up empty and I felt others were too. My most important goal became to help people like me – independent content creators – better understand the business of pitching. I set out to learn everything about pitching. I wanted to teach others what they needed to do to successfully pitch their projects to networks, agents, production companies, investors, and talent.

In order to write this book, I went on a couple of unpredictable, but rewarding, journeys. My first goal was to pitch 100 times so I could rise above the rejection and defeat I felt from hearing "we pass." My second goal was to learn to master the art of pitching. In order to do this, I had to step past my fears and learn to ask for big favors. Initially, I set out to ask 30 favors that on a normal day I would be too afraid to do. The challenge was amazing and transformative for me. On just day two of my big ask challenge, I realized that without representation I'd first have to muster up the confidence to ask executives for a pitch meeting. In order for the meetings to be successful, I was going to have to interview a lot of professionals who could answer my questions about pitching. If I was going to grow and realize my dream of creating for film and television, I needed to build enough courage to ask questions. And so my journey began.

Many of you may feel clueless about where to begin your pitch, or may not have any clue at all what to do in a pitch. If you are like me, you may have done research and come up short – maybe it's because you really aren't sure what to search for. You just know you have a great idea and want to sell it.

Some of you may be clueless about what a *bible* is and too afraid to ask questions about how to create a bible of any kind. You may not feel confident enough or knowledgeable enough of the industry, and are unsure of the buzzwords. Many of you may find yourself wondering, *"Where do I start my pitch?"* You may not want people to look at you like you are a novice. Don't let your ego stop you from doing the very thing we are passionate about. You have a fantastic idea and want to pitch it.

All of these are just a few of the questions that may have stopped you from pitching. If you can identify with any of these fears, keep reading. I hope to relieve you of all these fears by answering your questions, and hopefully you will walk away confident in your understanding of the step-by-step process as you begin your pitching journey.

In this book, I share the mistakes I've made since my first pitch in 2013 to today. I profile independent content creators and filmmakers who have bridged the gap. I also interview executives from BET, OWN, NBC, and ASPIRE TV production companies and others in the industry to gain insight on the dos and don'ts of pitching. What you learn will help you get rid of that fearful little voice in your head, or at least silence it when it creeps in, because you will be confident that you know all that you need to for a successful pitch.

CHAPTER ONE
Learn From These Mistakes

It's not how we make mistakes,
but how we correct them that defines us.
—Rachel Wolchin

Top Ten Common Mistakes Content Creators Make

Mistakes. We all make them, but the difference between people who win and lose is how they apply the lessons learned from the mistakes they've made. Mistakes are opportunities for growth. I have made many pitching mistakes. In all honesty, I didn't realize quite a few of my own mistakes until I began interviewing executives for this book. In retrospect, I realize that passion for my projects mixed with a natural instinct for developing stories allowed me to go to the next steps in my pitches. But what I have learned since I've been on my journey of pitching 100 times, and from talking to my interviewees, is the difference between getting in the doors and closing the deal.

It was in my interview with Endyia Kenney Sterns, former Vice President of Programming and development at OWN, that I first felt exposed. Endyia, though she didn't know it, made me reconsider pitching networks first. After meeting with her to get her insight for this book, I redirected my attention to pitching production companies after she said, "No one should be pitching a network if they haven't packaged their show." She was very clear that networks, OWN anyway, didn't have time to do the work for the content creator. *"Isn't that what the development team is for?"* I remember thinking. But she was right, and it's not only at OWN that this principle applies, it's at most networks.

That's when I realized that though I'd been lucky to get in a few doors over my pitching journey without doing any packaging, lack of packaging was most likely the reason many of my projects hadn't come to fruition. They didn't have enough viable appeal. I decided I should continue my pitching journey by partnering first with production companies to help me package, if I wasn't going to attach well-known talent myself. Going straight to a network or production house could jeopardize your opportunity if another project that is just as great is packaged and therefore more appealing. This is one of many lessons I grew from during my pitching journey.

Many of the mistakes I have made are pretty common. Maybe you too are making these big pitching mistakes, and that is why I have decided to highlight them in this first chapter: the only way to get our ideas green lit is to know where we are erring first and then learn how to correct our mistakes. Below are many of the common mistakes content creators make when pitching their ideas.

Pitching Concepts

It's a waste of time for the buyer (referring to whoever is optioning your idea, a network, studio house, or production company), when you only have a concept. It tells them you haven't taken the time to think through your idea. It leaves them to think you want them to do it for you. Who do you expect will want to create your project for you, the development department? I know that some of you may be thinking, *"I don't want to waste my time writing a script and creating a project that the network doesn't want."* Well, if you don't believe in your idea that early in advance, why should they? If you put the shoe on the other foot, would you want someone to waste your time this way?

Spend more time fleshing out your idea so that you've developed it from a simple concept through to a fully developed idea. Once you have completed this process and pitched the idea, if the development team decides to option your project they will further develop the idea, expounding on what you've created and making it fit with their network's or production company's mandate.

Reading from the Paper

Don't judge me. I made this mistake a few times before. I credit my expert storytelling to a harsh lesson I learned from Robert Townsend, (*Five Heartbeats*, and *Hollywood Shuffle*) after reading my pitch to him. This is an enormously common problem with content creators; they read the information right from the paper. The problem with reading from the paper is that there is no excitement or passion. There is something about listening to someone tell a story and going on a journey with them as they make discoveries while telling it. With each new idea that the storyteller presents, the listener goes on an imaginative journey with the storyteller. Eliminating the paper from your pitches will help to keep the buyer engaged and in tune with you as you share information about your project. Otherwise, you could have emailed the information to them and let them read it. I heard someone once say *the art is in the heart*. The point for getting an in-person meeting is to engage them with what is in your heart, not with what is not on the paper.

Not Packaging Your Projects

I didn't understand the term *packaging* when I first began pitching. I blindly went into pitching. I had an idea that I'd developed. That was it. The term *packaging*, for those who don't know, means to attach actors, writers, directors, and producers to your project. The bigger understanding is that someone has liked your idea enough to say, "Yes." This "yes" is what networks, studios, or production companies hear when they learn you have packaged your project. That yes is what penetrates the proverbial wall (built to keep content creators without representation out) and sends it tumbling down. You need a yes or two.

Quick story. I had a friend who worked to create a reality hair show with a hairstylist. My friend sent in her sizzle reel [a pitch video that sells the overview of a project in 3-5 minutes], to someone she knew at a production company and weeks later the company contacted her with some interesting news: a network had reached out to them with an idea very similar in nature to hers. The only difference was that the other project had *named*, or celebrity talent, attached. She was very bothered by this, and it's an easy experience to learn and grow from. In order to make your project more viable, and potentially maintain control, you have to package your project so that it has strong appeal to networks, studios, and investors. A network development executive once told me that there are only seven types of stories out there. They just have different leading characters and different worlds. This means your project better be the one with the most worthwhile attractiveness. To make it worthwhile, you have to package it so that it has the most viable appeal.

Not Building Relationships

Relationship building is everything to pitching. How much easier do you think it would be to get in the door if you knew the head of development at a network, production company, or studio? But many people, with titles that may not relate to anything that indicates development, could be a major factor in helping you gain access to the right person, so you want to learn to treat everyone with respect. You never know, the cleaning lady, the mailman, the person who works as a driver for Domino's pizza, or the assistant to a development executive could all be of value; they could be the one who connects you to their family member or friend who is in development. In fact, the assistant is a very important person to know. One should always get to know the gatekeepers and build a respectful relationship with them. But most people do the opposite.

A friend of mine was assistant to the president of a production company. Every day, the president of the company would have her vet the content creators and their projects first before passing them over to the next

4

person in rotation, which in many cases was the president. She told me that many of the people who were trying to gain access, who didn't have representation, would treat her disrespectfully, especially once they learned that their initial pitch meeting was with her. They would email the president back and ask to be seen by someone else, or they would treat her as if she didn't have the knowledge and expertise to understand if their project was any good. The assistant, a content creator herself, has projects that have won awards and been licensed on network television. She hasn't made it quite yet, but has worked in development at other networks and has a great understanding of development. This assistant eventually went to the president and asked him to change her title so the people wouldn't treat her so badly. The president said, "If they treat you badly, then 'pass' on their projects. I don't want to do business with someone like them anyway." And so there were quite a few rejections handed out, solely on attitude alone.

As I said earlier in this book, I spent more than a year building a relationship with the executive for *Being Bobby Brown.* I continue to stay in touch with her. I comment on her Snapchats, I like Facebook posts, and I email to schedule lunches simply to catch up. I remain in contact with other people in the industry too. I don't only come to them when I need something. I reach out to them to fill a need, or to check on them if I've learned on social media something went wrong; I send holiday wishes, check on them if a tornado or hurricane was near where they live; or simply check in to see how they are doing. I work to build the relationship into one I envision having with them.

So how do you begin a relationship with people in the industry? There is a way you can get to know the people you eventually want to pitch: it's called research. There are so many ways you can learn more about people. There is IMDBpro – I always start my research there to get the names of the executives. Another way is through LinkedIn. LinkedIn is usually my second resource. You can connect with investors, a person at a network, a production company, and talent that may not be in development but can lead you to all of the people at that company, agency, studio, or network. Get to know more about your prospects through social media. Social media can tell you much about a person and their company or network they work for. If you can, first connect with them, learn more about them, socialize with them, and then see how you can pitch them.

Not Making Your Content Fit the Network

This is another mistake I made early on. My partner and I were determined to sell a drama that we'd created to a network. This year, 2014, the head of development at Aspire TV was holding pitch meetings at the American Black Film Festival (ABFF); we had met the head of development and already established a relationship with her. She allowed us to pitch her last and at our request agreed to include the general manager in the meeting.

Once in the meeting, the general manager wanted to get to know us, so he began asking us questions about our previous work and personal lives. The questions were light, nothing major, but we weren't expecting to…well…talk! For the first 10 minutes of the 20 she'd promised us with the general manager, we talked about seemingly everything, and yet nothing. Then once he was ready, we delved into our pitch about our hour-long drama.

It's important that I give you a little background about Aspire TV so you can understand why our pitch was so wrong for the network. The network, started by Magic Johnson, had only launched in 2013. When they launched, they did so after acquiring a program full of older shows like *The Cosby Show*, *Flip Wilson*, and other older movies. The newest programming they had was *ABFF Independent*, a show full of short films they were showcasing that they also used as part of their launch. One of the short films I produced was a part of that launch. A year later they were seeking to expand their programming with newer content and that is why they were holding pitch meetings. When my writing partner and I pitched our drama, it was only after a year of launching the network. It's 2016 and the network is still not quite ready to put money into a drama that would cost at least a million dollars per episode.

So, our content was not right for who we were pitching at the time. They loved our pitch, but politely told us to come back in four–five years when they'd be ready to put money into an original drama. If we were more knowledgeable back then, we would have created a cheaper show, perhaps even a reality or digital show that was perfect for their network, and pitched it. See the importance of doing your research before pitching? You could waste their and your time pitching them the wrong thing.

Pitching via Email

Someone shared with me via LinkedIn that he was sending written pitches to distributors and sales agents. "Written pitches?" I asked him. "What does that consist of?" He explained that he was literally pitching via email. He sent me copies of his pitch emails, which had all of the information he'd say at an in-person pitch, but in a very well-crafted email. The good thing is, he is really a great writer. However, for many reasons I'd say this is more wrong than right.

First know that many companies won't even read an email pitch because it's considered *unsolicited material*, and they are too afraid of getting sued for copyright infringement if a similar idea comes through their door that they send to series. But, that's their reason and not mine. I'm certainly the type of person who will challenge companies to break that rule in an attempt to hear more fresh voices, to hear my fresh voice! My reason to not send an email pitch EVER is that you completely shut yourself out of the possibility of persuasion. What is written on paper, no matter how excellent, cannot deliver the same as it would if you were saying it in person. One thing is undeniable, that is your passion about your project. *Paper ain't got no passion!* Also, executives aren't always the creative type. Granted, there are a few who come from a background of content creation and managed to get jobs in corporate; they could probably see your vision. But, that may not always be the case and you are leaving your gem of creation to them and their minds. Good project. Good opportunity. Gone bad.

In your email, you should give enough information to entice the reader to make an appointment to learn more and save the rest for the room. Sending an email pitch allows the executive to pass on your project without any creative input from you. So, if you are email pitching, cease and desist! In Chapter 5, I will discuss how to write emails that entice.

Not Rehearsing Your Pitch

Sigh. Yes, even I have made this mistake before. One would think that this is a no brainer – of course everyone would logically rehearse his or her pitch. You'd be surprise how many people do not rehearse before they pitch. Some people think because they created the content they know the material by rote. Do you know how many times I've forgotten loglines? Character names? Themes? Most of the time, it was my nerves getting the best of me, but with many projects floating around in my head, sometimes I have everything mixed up. Worse, many people go into pitch meetings not rehearsing with their team or talent. So, when questions are asked to the team, they are speaking at the same time because neither has decided who would answer what questions. If you are bringing talent into the room with you, they may not know how to answer some of the questions, or may not be familiar with some aspects of your show and are left looking dumbfounded. The biggest reason to rehearse your pitch is you never know if you will only end up with five minutes to say what you have to say or 30 minutes, and you want to be ready in both situations. Chapter 4 is dedicated to practicing the pitch so that you can be prepared for every situation. In fact, I suggest quite a few ways to practice your pitch throughout this book as well as many pitching challenges so that you can be prepared for all situations. You will have worked your project out so many ways you could pitch your way out of any box if you need to. Rehearsing your pitch kicks these kinds of issues in the butt.

Asking for a Non-Disclosure Agreement (NDA)

To ask or not to ask, that is *always* the question for an independent, underrepresented content creator. It's a topic that distresses me greatly and is a sore topic for the independent creative. While I can't tell you which way is best, I can say that after making a mistake and asking for one and that deal going sour after asking, I do not ask for them anymore. You see, four years ago after my very first pitch – just days after receiving "next steps" from the network – I received earth-shattering news: they decided to pass. I truly believe it was because I'd asked them to sign an NDA.

Chapter 7 will give more insight into the reasons why networks and production companies cringe at signing NDAs. I'll let you decide for yourself after reading the interview I had with former Senior Director at BET Network, Austyn Biggers, who is now Executive Producer of Development at Logo TV. Austyn passed on our pitch after I asked him to sign an NDA. I specifically returned to him to ask about NDAs because I wanted to confirm my belief about the reason they had passed. I'll let you be the judge.

Harassing the Executives

This is a mistake I never made, thank God! But, I know people who ride a fine line of harassment when it comes to connecting with and following up with executives. After you have pitched or before you have pitched, for that matter, please put yourself in the shoes of the person you are seeking to build a long-lasting relationship with. Ask yourself, "*If I were on the other end of this email or phone, what kind of person would I want to build a relationship with, someone who is patient and understands how busy my workload can be and can respect my time and maybe even my silence? Or would I want to build a relationship with someone who is so persistent they will call and email until I pick up the phone or until I give them a final answer, no matter how many emails and calls it takes?*" Unfortunately, someone's silence may mean they aren't interested. Either way, you need to respect it. I personally like to wait at least two–three weeks before following up unless specifically told to do otherwise. Aside from letting executives know when something major has happened in my life, or that I have recently completed another project, or simply to do some relationship building, I don't reach out to them. I like to respect the working relationship. Your goal should be to establish a long-lasting relationship with them, and respecting their time and decision is the first key to building the relationship.

Overselling the Project

Another mistake that content creators often make is forecasting what will happen when the world views their work. "You are going to love it, it's amazing!" or, "My show will move the hearts of many" or, "It's a show that will make millions want to tune in!"

When selling your project, don't offer your opinion or predict what the viewer will do or say about the project because you can't determine how people will respond. Stick to the facts about your project, not your opinion, and instead of telling them they will love it, offer them answers for what, why, and how they will love your project. The hoopla is great and is really enticing, but at the end of the day, if you haven't answered what your story is about then you've wasted their time and yours. Leave the fluff out of the pitch and pitch the facts.

Pitching Challenge #1

So, you have an idea you want to pitch. I'm not really concerned at this point where you are in your creative process; whether it is simply a concept or if you have fully thought your idea through, (though you will want to in the end), I want you to stop what you're doing and do an impromptu pitch.

Yep, you heard right. ***This is a pitching challenge.***

Right now, pull out a recording device, hit record, and pitch your concept. Do not think much about it; just pitch now. You can use your phone or any other kind of recording device. I use a recording app called REV because I can upload it to Dropbox and have it transcribed right from the app if I need to. Plus, I like to have it on all of my mobile devices when I am ready to listen to it. You can use whatever device works best for you, though, even if it is an old-school tape recorder. Press record and sell your concept; pitch your idea.

I'm serious. STOP reading this and pitch your idea to the recorder. It's just you and the recorder, no reason to stress over it.

GO!

Now, that wasn't so bad (or was it?). I know I put you on the spot. But truth be told, some of your pitches will happen on the spot with no time to prepare. At some point on your pitching journey, you will run into someone who can help take your concept to the next level, and you will have to sell them on your show or film idea. What you just did is a clear indication of how ready you are to pitch your project.

Now that we got that out of the way, don't delete the recording. The real purpose of that pitching challenge was to use it as a metric for growth. Periodically, while reading this book, I will give you pitching challenges and instructions that will challenge you and the way you pitch your project. In addition to learning from my and other people's mistakes, my goal is for you to apply the pitching strategies and case studies taught in this book. If you do this, I believe by the end of this book your pitch will be succinct and compelling. If you can accomplish creating a winning pitch, then I have done my job! Ready?

CHAPTER TWO
Development

*The best way to show my thanks to God is to do my
very best with the talents he's given me.*
—Siri Lindley

#1 My First Pitch...Ever

BET (Black Entertainment Television)

My first pitch was with BET in March of 2013. I reached out to the president of BET. Yeah...I had some big balls. I didn't care; I was feeling great this day and I decided to take a risk. In full disclosure, at the time I was working at Viacom in New York in the mergers and acquisitions department. I had been temping as an executive assistant with the company for about five months when I decided to send this email to the president. It's what added to my risk taking; I could potentially have risked my job doing that, as I didn't know what rules there were around pitching within the company. I didn't know how long my stint would be there and knew I needed to use the job as an opportunity. Originally, I contacted her because I was seeking an executive producer for a drama series I was co-writing with a partner. I sent the then president, Loretha Jones, an email describing how wonderful a "trail-blazer" she was and described my project in brief. She responded that same day and informed me that her job was her sole professional focus, but she suggested that we pitch our project to them and she cc'd the then senior director, Austyn Biggers. I was amazed that she responded to my email! I was through my first door at BET!

I reached out to my writing partner to let her know that we had our first offer to pitch. Neither my partner nor I lived in Los Angeles. I lived in New York and she lived in Atlanta, Georgia at that time. Neither of us had money readily available to travel to LA, so I asked when we should set a date to pitch him. We gave ourselves two and a half weeks to get to LA and pitch. I followed up with Austyn and offered him availability that spanned a week long, stating, "My partner and I will be in LA next month, [it was February 27th] any chance you are free to meet during the week of the March 20th?" I figured he had to be available sometime during the entire week. He was. We set up a meeting day and time.

Guess how prepared we were for the pitch?

Not at all prepared. At this point we sort of had a concept in mind. Our idea wasn't fully fleshed out; we weren't completely sure which direction we were going in. We knew we wanted to base the series off of the short film we shot the year prior, and we had a logline based on some of its themes, but that is literally all we had – a concept. Nothing else. So, now we were facing two weeks to develop an episodic and to write a pilot episode, and half a week to practice our pitch and fly to LA.

We spent the following days and nights brainstorming ideas to sculpt the world of the show and characters. We began putting information into a Word document. At the time, we weren't knowledgeable enough about the industry buzzwords to know that we were creating a show bible. We were simply dumping all of our ideas into this document along with pictures of prototypes of people who we thought would play the roles. We worked relentlessly on a series we could be proud of. It took us about a week and a half to create our series. We also created a 70-page pilot script in the following days, finishing up the night before it was time to fly out. Neither of us was experienced with doing PowerPoint decks at that time, so I asked a friend who worked in marketing at NBC if she could help us create one. We rehearsed our pitch with her over the phone and she gave us critiques on what worked and what was unclear. We flew to LA the next morning and there we continued to work on our pitch deck and script. We rehearsed once more with our marketing friend over the phone and felt we were as ready as we would ever be for our pitch.

We waited with bated breath after pitching Austyn and received some rave reviews. Austyn paid several compliments to us; the greatest was that the world of our show was well thought-out. He said, "Many people create amazing characters but forget to create the world of the show." Austyn asked questions about our characters – relationship questions that we hadn't thought of – but because we understood the relationships well, we were able to come up with answers on the spot.

Looking back, I'm sure he could tell we were novice creators who hadn't pitched before; if nothing else, because of the length of time we took to pitch and how we went about pitching, but we had done our jobs creatively and delivered a great story. Austyn told us that although the network recently picked up two different shows with similar themes for development, he really loved our show and wanted to bring us back in to pitch to his team. He asked us if we had written a pilot episode or if we planned to get writers. We told him we had written the pilot ourselves. He suggested we send it and our bible to him by email once we returned home so his team could review it. He was gracious enough to offer his time to help us better prepare for his team before we met with them.

To this day, I feel I owe him for his help; yet, he wouldn't be the first executive to treat my various writing partners and me with great respect. Over the years, I would learn to stop looking at the buyers as the great Wizards of Oz, and realize they were human; some were creative, and just as in need as I was. I would grow to understand that they needed creatives like me just as much as I needed them. Over the course of my journey, this eye-opening lesson took some of my pitching fears away.

Once we returned home, my partner and I decided to have a lawyer draw up a Non-Disclosure Agreement (NDA) and had him send it to Austyn asking for signatures before we sent over our materials. The deal went sour.

While there is so much to discuss regarding our first pitch – the world of a project, writing emails, and NDA's – I'll leave it for future chapters in this book. For now, I want to discuss some lessons learned from our first pitch. The above is a great story of a first pitch and truly we had some wins here. But in retrospect, we made a few mistakes that many who are new to the game of pitching can learn from.

Takeaways

The first takeaway from the story above is *DON'T TRY THIS AT HOME*! You should be fully prepared *before* you reach out to pitch anyone. We were lucky. Yes, we had a great story, but we were lucky that I worked at Viacom and had an in with the development team. We were lucky that I didn't get fired because I sure as hell wouldn't have had a TV show on air after the pitch! We were lucky that Austyn Biggers has a heart for independent content creators and women, and that he allowed us to take up a little over an hour of his time because that is not typical of how long you are usually given in a pitch meeting. We were lucky that he was willing to give us a mini-lesson on pitching the higher-ups at BET; training on the job is not the norm in the pitching world. We were lucky to have done so much in so little time without being stricken with writer's block. We were truly lucky.

Our pitch worked because we designed a good show with great characters. We understood every single element of the show. There weren't many questions the executive could ask us that we hadn't thought through. We even came up with marketing ideas and cross-promotional ideas. This pitch worked because our creative abilities, jointly, brought about a pretty well-developed show.

Our script, a 70-page first draft, would have been our biggest bomb had we not asked for a non-disclosure agreement first. We were lucky he hadn't asked for any materials in the room that day because we could have not only lost the deal, but also lost his respect for our writing skills: that script was nowhere close to being ready. We hadn't even had time to check for errors. After the pitch meeting, we went back into rewrites and found many mistakes, and as a first draft, the script was in bad shape. The script could have ruined the deal for us if it hadn't already gone sour.

You want to hand over your materials confident that they are your absolute best.

Also, you can never know what documents they will request after your pitch. It varies person-to-person and network-to-network, so you want to be ready for whatever they ask for. You don't want to return home and have to write several drafts of a script or create a pitch bible. That takes time, and you don't want the executives to have to wait for materials. They may be interested today and tomorrow their mandate or directives could change. What if someone else comes in with an idea, not like yours, but with the same themes as yours, and because they are prepared, they are able to hand over the materials before you can hand over yours? That could potentially cause you to get a "we're going to pass" on your project. Additionally, if you only come with a concept and the person you are pitching asks you several questions you haven't thought through yet, and you can't answer them, it could sour a potential deal.

Networks, investors, producers, directors, and actors are only able to take on a certain number of new projects each year, and if they are being pitched by hundreds of others – they most likely are – then your first impression had better be your best impression! You want to go in pitch perfect.

Believe it or not, many people pitch concepts, celebrities do it too! Well, what separates you from the rest of the people who only have concepts? I can tell you. A well-developed idea. Yes, in many cases you may be pitching a development department, but they don't want to do the work for you. Your job as a content creator is to be as developed as you can be; the development team helps you further develop what you have for their network if your pitch is optioned.

An executive for Monami Entertainment expressed interest in two of my projects after pitching him. I asked him how long it would take to go to next steps should they decide to option either of my projects. He said since my ideas were developed, he thought it would only take about three months to complete development on the project and that would be simply to package it. I then asked how long it typically takes to develop a project, and he said anywhere from 6-12 months. He was impressed that I had fully developed my projects. I believe he respects me as a serious content creator now, even though the deal didn't work out between Monami and me. This impression precedes me and will certainly help me get through those doors again should another idea develop that I think they would be interested in.

If you only come with a concept, how should the buyer know that you could follow through and fully develop the project? Why should they gamble on an idea that dropped into your head? Being unprepared speaks volumes about where you are on your journey of pitching; are you a novice, a professional, or are you somewhere in between? No matter where you are on the spectrum, you want to be as buttoned up and as prepared as you can be.

How to Know You Are Ready to Pitch

All content creators should fully develop their projects before pitching to a buyer. Therefore, I think it's important to write about the development process. It's easy to come up with concepts. Concepts drop into people's minds daily; some of them are really good, yet the concept never goes any further than across their minds. The buyer will want to know if you can develop your idea completely, from concept to fruition. That's one reason why they ask for a bible. It shows them that you have thought through the various elements of your project. I believe it's impossible to pitch successfully without fully developing your project. Don't get me wrong, once your project is optioned there will still be development that will take place with the network or studio and their development teams, but your full idea should be penned in detail so that you are able to answer the many questions asked by the curious buyer and their teams. If you develop your project it will ensure you are completely buttoned up and ready for the pitching process.

I understand, however, that many of you have amazing ideas and want to do the work to bring them to fruition, but you may feel overwhelmed about where to start creating them. I've created a mind mapping process that will help you develop your project and later create pitching materials.

From Concept to Creation

Let's say a concept drops into your head that you think is an amazing idea and you want to take it further. The first thing I suggest doing is mind mapping your project to simplify it! Sometimes a film, TV, or digital project is too big to look at as a whole. It's overwhelming. So, what you need to do is break it down into categories by doing a mind map. I've developed a mind mapping process below for you to use:

1) Start by writing the title of your project in the center of a page.
2) Then begin your brainstorm. Draw lines from whatever idea comes to mind about your title. This is where you don't hold back; just write your thoughts freely without editing anything. Saying no to any idea at this stage in the game could be deadly to your project.
3) In order to make sure your mind map is multi-layered and bible ready, you want to brainstorm the following: characters, themes, scenes, locations, moods, background, style elements, logline ideas, episodes, fears, goals, and relationships.
4) Ask yourself the following questions to make sure you are making multi-dimensional characters and a multi-dimensional world:
   1. What is my show about?
   2. How is this show different from others that are similar? You definitely want to speak about this when pitching your project. Pitching what makes it different from others similar to it will ensure you stand out from the others in its category.
   3. Who are the main characters?
   4. What makes them unique? Interesting? How do they differ from the others in my show?
   5. What are their fears?
   6. What are their secrets and who do they want to keep from finding out?
   7. Who would play them?
   8. How are my characters connected to each other?
   9. What are their relationships like with the others?
   10. Where does this project take place?
   11. What do the locations look like?
   12. What are the rules of my show, if any?
   13. What audience will it attract? Why?
   14. How can I make this project multi-dimensional?
   15. How could this show be marketed?
   16. What are the chapters in each character's life?
   17. What are possible titles?
   18. What situations do these characters find themselves in?
   19. If you could flashback to defining moments of your characters' past, what moments would be pivotal?

After you are done, draw a circle around all of the ideas that are similar or that would fall into the same category. After you have drawn your circle, give each circle a category, then further break it down to give each category a title, and bullet each idea within the circle under each title. If something else comes to mind, write it as another bullet. Your mind map may look like the one pictured below. An example of a bulleted list is included after.

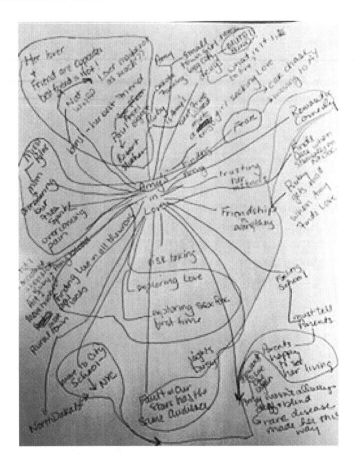

Example:

1. Titles:
   - Finding Amy
   - Amy finds love
2. Stories I want to tell:
   - Learning of her illness
   - Meeting Ruby

- Her move to NYC
- My first horrible incident living blind and mute in NYC

3. Act 1:
   - Her and Ruby become blood buddies
   - Her illness

4. Act 2:
   - Moving to NYC
   - Meeting Paul
   - Falling in love

Spend time mind mapping your project. It will help focus your thoughts and get your ideas on paper. Also, the project won't seem so overwhelming after you've mind mapped it. After you have mind mapped and created your categories, it's time to add the information to a document that will end up being your bible.

CHAPTER THREE
Developing the Story

Preparation begets confidence.
—Squeaky Moore

The Pitching Checklist

How many of you are guilty of going into a pitch meeting with only a concept?

A content creator asked me *after* she'd pitched a network, "How do I prepare to get a 'yes,' and 'how do I seal the deal?'" Her questions didn't surprise me at all. It's what many ambitious, talented content creators do all the time. We just go for it. Blindly. This particular creative went with the opportunity that came her way, with a concept that wasn't entirely fleshed out. She used her instinct and passion to pitch her project. She went in strong, and came out of the meeting reeling with questions. *How did that go? What do they think? Did I say all the right things? Should I have done this? Should I have said that? When will I hear back? What do I do now to get them to say "Yes"?*

I had many of my own questions after reading her message. Among them, the first question I needed to know in order to help her was, "*How did you prepare?*" Her question, "*How do I prepare to get a 'yes'*" was misplaced. It was a question that should have been asked before the meeting, right? I wondered a few more: *did she pitch only a concept or was the idea completely developed? What did she say in her pitch?* Most importantly, *what did they say at the end of the meeting?* There was no way I could answer her without knowing these questions first. But her question, "How should I prepare to get a 'yes'?" sent an alarm.

Again, I want to say I've done this before, pitching without fully being prepared. But, if I knew then what I know now, I could have saved time, relationships, and established more trust. Everyone should "prepare to get a yes," as best they can *before* they go in to pitch. When we get our lucky shot, everything is hinging on it. We only get one chance most of the time to impress the people we are pitching. Most of the time there aren't any redo's. We have to "seal the deal" at the first opportunity. In reality, there aren't any preliminary rounds; the first meeting can be the knockout round if you aren't completely buttoned up and ready to impress them with everything they need to know for you to bring home a "yes."

After getting more information, I learned that the content creator had a pretty cool concept. However, it wasn't fleshed out enough to go into pitch meetings. She'd only had the concept and the pilot episode in her pitching materials. Also, the materials she was using (or at least what was sent to me) had other concepts she was selling in the same document. It took me a few read-throughs after getting excited about the concept to clearly understand that what followed were completely different ideas. To those of you thinking about going into a pitch meeting without fully fleshing out your idea, STOP and slow down. I want you to be better prepared. I want to help you fully realize your idea and have it all fleshed out.

I created a pitching checklist to help you know when you are adequately prepared to pitch so that you can seal the deal on your first meeting. If you do these steps you will know you are prepared to start making calls, sending emails, and pitching.

Here is what you need to do to be fully prepared to pitch:

1) Create a Pitch Bible and/or Treatment

Start here. After you have done a mind map of your project, it's time to develop it thoroughly. The first thing you should do is create a pitch bible. In short, a pitch bible (sometimes called a show bible for television networks) is a document used to help create and communicate your story idea, and help the buyer (the network or studio house), understand your concept as you see it. Constructing a bible is the best development tool you can use for your project. Making a pitch or format bible, or treatment, will ensure you know everything about your project from loglines to episodes to story arc and voice syntax! Add as much information into your bible as you can to make sure anyone reading it will see exactly what you envision. Creating a bible says I have more than just a concept: I fully understand the story and characters I am selling. It will help you to know where your story is going. The bible helps the buyer to understand the arc of the series or film, its mood and tone, and the setting of your story. If it's on a beach, is it in New York or California? (Those are completely different beaches and you should be specific in your description of them.) Your specificity in the bible will sell your idea and help the buyer carry your idea out as envisioned and sell it to others. All writers and show creators should get in a habit of creating a bible whether anyone ever sees it or not. Then it does not matter what questions producers, investors, or development executives ask because you will most likely have the answer. If picked up, a team of writers and producers will need to use the bible to create episodes for seasons to come and it will serve as the blueprint.

If you are creating a pitch bible you will need to include the following:

Title page

Believe it or not, titles carry a lot of weight! One guy once told me he didn't go see *Clear and Present Danger* because the title annoyed him. The title! Can you believe that someone would not go to see a film simply because the title didn't work for them? Well, it's true and it makes a lot of sense to me now, no matter how subjective it all can end up being. I remember when the Wayans brothers came out with, (and I still have to look up the title of this film before saying it), *Don't Be a Menace to South Central While Drinking Your Juice in the Hood.* I know it's just a parody film, but the title is one that stopped me from seeing it. The title reads as frolicsome and being for someone looking for cheap laughs, which probably fits its genre. I just couldn't bring myself to see the film and I like the Wayan brothers. Shonda Rhimes is someone who has done well with titles, like *Scandal, Grey's Anatomy,* and *How To Get Away With Murder.* Other examples of titles that have worked well, for me anyway, that capture the projects content well are *Inside Out, Gotham, Sex and the City,* and *Power,* to name a few.

Titles are important to a project. That's why you see so many "working titles" because people are still trying to figure out the best one for the project. It wasn't until I heard show creator Alexis de Gemini say the title of your project should encapsulate its environment that I realized just how many title mistakes I was making. Before then, I'd created some very catchy titles for my projects, which were in retrospect, pretty gimmicky. I chose titles for my projects by cleverly playing on the words, though sometimes the title had nothing really to do with the themes or environment of my story. This wasn't in my best interest. It is important to think of the audience you want to view your film when considering a title. Will they get it if you play on the words? Maybe so. Maybe not. One thing's for sure, 50/50 is too much of a gamble.

I was teaching a workshop once and a content creator told us the title of her script. When we all fell silent, she went on to explain why she chose the title. Her explanation was gimmicky, too. If you have to explain your title, it probably isn't the one for the project. The cover art and promotional materials won't have enough space for your explanation and you won't be able to explain your reasons to the rest of the world. So, make sure your title can stand on its own. A title can negatively influence the mind of someone you are pitching.

I read an article in an issue of *The New Yorker* about STX's Entertainment Chairman, Alex Fogelson. In it, he mentions how the title of a project made it seem "indie." His statement reminded me of the importance of a title. It also made me aware of how executives think and how much the odds are truly stacked against the independent creator, lacking representation, if we aren't thinking about the finest details. As an independent content creator, we must think on a broader scale when creating; we must think like *they* think. When I read the title, I had to agree that I could see why he thought that way. Referring to the movie, *The Gift*, it read,

> With "The Gift," Fogelson had no spectacle to sell – only the film's premise. "The movie's original title was 'Weirdo,' which sounds indie, so we changed that," he said. He didn't want people thinking the film was weird; he wanted them thinking it was creepy.[2]

Reading this article taught me to always consider my project's premise and world when creating a title and leave the gimmicky stuff out – that is, of course, unless your play on words really does work well with the core idea you are creating.

Ask yourself, *"What do I **want** people to walk away thinking when they read the title of my project?"* Create a list of the words you come up with. Now ask yourself, *"Does my title make people think [insert words from your list]?"*

Logline

The logline has been written about so much on the Internet that I almost felt it redundant to write about it in this book. But as I studied what made a great logline and compared it to the loglines I'd written in the past, I realized it was worth it to give this subject a little of my time as I had made tremendous mistakes creating them in the past.

I'll start by making clear what a logline isn't. It isn't a tag line, a short catchy phrase or slogan that you may find on the cover art of a film. I realized that many content creators think they are one and the same, but they aren't. Nor is a logline the premise (events that set the story into action), which I had mistakenly used in the past to create some of my loglines. The logline is one–two sentences that sell what your project is about. It's an important element of the bible. The logline should summarize the whole of your project with all of its multiple layers into

---

[2] Tad Friend, "The Mogul of The Middle," *The New Yorker*, January 11, 2016, http://www.newyorker.com/magazine/2016/01/11/the-mogul-of-the-middle

one succinct sentence, or two sentences at the most. Think of it as your short pitch, the one you may use in an elevator. In that short ride, you want to make sure your short sale encompasses the whole of your project while hooking the reader, viewer, and in this case, the buyer.

The logline should have some structure to it or at least follow the guidelines that include the five basic story elements. By basic elements, I don't mean who, what, when, where, and why, although it most likely will include those things. Your logline should include, in no particular order, your lead character, genre, goal or objective, the conflict and the stake of your project. After you have included the five basic elements in your logline, go back to see if the five Ws are included, and if not, see if you can also include them all into this one–two sentence logline.

The second part is used to tighten up your logline. Creating the logline will probably take just as much time as it does to write the script. Well, maybe not as long, but you should spend some time here trying to include all of the five elements. Your logline will also help guide you to stay on subject while writing the script. It's extremely important because it's your calling card for getting in the door. You will most likely use it many times on many of the pitch materials you create, including the bible, one-sheet, in emails, and in person. So, it's best to put in the time creating a great one that can stand and win on its own.

This is my final note on the logline. I have created loglines that do not include the genre; sometimes the genre can be implied in the logline by how it is written. In other words, a content creator can imply the genre by its tone. I was working with a content creator on her logline for a girl comedy and I'd taken a page of the most important details of her show and brainstormed about four different loglines. When we discussed my brainstorm, one of the loglines, which seemed the best, ended up being one we couldn't use because the tone of it made it feel like her girl comedy was a drama. After much discussion, we'd decided to delete a phrase that was making it feel dramatic, which was "harsh realities." That phrase was not right for the comedy she'd written. Additionally, we added a two-word religious title to the girl, which implied that she was a fish out of water. Those two adjustments changed the tone of her logline, adding a comedic feel to it.

Premise

It is important to understand the premise of your story, as one may choose to begin their pitch starting with the premise and move forward with telling the story from that point. The premise is one or two sentences about what happened before your story begins. It answers the question, "how did the story come to be?" In other words, it serves as the underpinning for the idea of your story. It's what sets the story up and makes the story continue, leaving out all that happens in between and at the end of it.

For example, the premise of *E.T* would be an alien is stranded on earth and becomes friends with a young boy. In another example, one might say the premise of Lena Dunham's, *Girls* is a post-graduate student being forced to face the realities of adulthood after her parents cut her off financially, or, four postgraduate students are forced to face the realities of adulthood. As you can see the premise of both the film and HBO's cable show are only what starts the journey of those stories.

Synopsis

The synopsis will explain everything that happens in your story moment to moment. The synopsis should have your characters' unique voices and be told throughout its one or two paragraphs using the mood and tone of your project. Unlike the premise, the synopsis should detail the complete story as well as what happens at the end of the story. When writing about the plot, introduce your main characters and their motivations. The synopsis should also mention the themes of your project.

Overview

The overview is a longer write-up of your complete story and development of the plot. Told in more of a story form, it includes all of the ideas of the story from the main characters – their arcs and what stands in their way – and the mood and tone of the story, which should show through the way this section is written. It should touch on the themes as well. Your overview should entice the reader to want to read on.

The biggest problem I had and continue to see with content creators writing overviews, synopsis, and/or treatments is that they forget to be creative! You can't throw your creativity out the window here after spending so much time creating your show or film. Don't simply talk about the facts of your script; rather, describe the build-up and intensity of the script as it reaches its climatic moments. If it is a film, you can build it up discussing the highs and lows of the character objectives, not forgetting the conflict. If it is a series, write about the premise of how the protagonist ends up where he or she is and discuss the arcs of the season – maybe your series' arc begins in episode 7 or 8, write about that high point. Paint a clear picture of the world of your show. Show how the viewer will connect with the universal themes. Viewers may not relate to a drug dealer, but they may relate to his need to want to have more in life. Or the viewer may not relate to or like horror, but may relate to racism, like in Jordan Peele's film, *Get Out*. So, write about the themes using the topics and experiences that are universal to a broader audience.

Show your attitude about each character by writing about them from their distinct perspectives. Your overview should include how you want the world to view each character individually. If your characters talk a certain way or if their syntax is unique, show it in the overview. In other words, if you were writing about Tommy in the hit show *Power*, on Starz, your wording wouldn't sound as if he is a good-natured White friend of Ghost. You would write him the only way a White man can be portrayed in an otherwise all-Black urban environment: hardcore; harder to the core than everyone else because Tommy has more to prove than the average man in the hood. This voice would then be juxtaposed with Ghost, whose syntax and demeanor may read opposite of that of a Black man, a kingpin, who grew up in the hood, because Ghosts' goal is to get out.

Writing the overview should be fun. If you are currently looking at it as the hardest task ever to create, reframe your thinking by remembering your *why*. Familiarize yourself with the passion that kept you up at night to write your script. I suggest recording audio of yourself simply telling someone about the story you have already scripted, then replay the audio to see what about your story was most appealing. It could be the way to begin your overview. Another tip is to think of peeling the wall back and giving a glimpse into the world of your character. Vince Gilligan, writer of *Breaking Bad*, does an amazing job of giving us a glimpse into the world of Walter White in his bible. His bible should be the standard that all content creators learn from. I will use quite a few examples of it in this chapter. The overview of Vince's bible follows:

> What I aim to tell is nothing less than the authoritative story of our nation's most famous and controversial substance: the drug. What are these popular chemicals? Who are the villains that produce them? Who are the heroes that volunteer to consume them? Who are the soldiers tasked with arresting an equal number of these heroes and villains?

Our window into this world? None other than Walter White, a disgusting man who has been bald since birth and is furious because he's a high school teacher. In his free time, he tries to drown his horrible students' cars at a local gas station – a task at which he always fails, to his mounting anger. On top of all this, Walter is battling a secret. Crippling addiction to pub trivia.[3]

Boy does he know how to entice! In his overview, you get a sense that "the drug" is a character, maybe even a leading one. However, what is most intriguing is how he shares his attitude about the characters in the show, looking at them as "villains," "soldiers," and "heroes." The main character is a villain, and the heroes are addicts – that is very clever. In addition, one gets a sense of the mood and tone of the show based on the bible. When creating your pitch materials, everything, I mean *everything* in your materials should replicate the mood of the project you have created.

Setting/Location

Simply writing the city and state to describe the setting and location of my script is a mistake I made too many times to mention. Have you done this? Have you written in your bible, "Set in Brooklyn, New York"? The problem with only giving this simple explanation of where your script is set is that a large population of the world may not be familiar with Brooklyn or the location as you see it in your mind's eye. When writing about setting and location, you can't forget to write about your perspective of the location, or at least the characters' perspective of it. Does the location have a stench? How does the creak in the wooden floor affect the character? Are the days of your character's life gloomy because of his impending death?

This part of the bible should explain what the person would see in the backdrop of where these characters exist. I have never lived in North Dakota, so if someone wrote, "Set in the rural areas of North Dakota," I would be at a loss and my mental imagery would simply be a white backdrop, or I would paint my own rural picture of what I think North Dakota looks like. Likewise, if your set is placed around a neighborhood of trailer homes, someone else may not have a clear depiction of what living in trailer homes is really like. You have to set the mood by setting up the location. My suggestion is to close your eyes and write how you envision your setting. Write what you want the viewer to see when they

---

[3] "This Is Vince Gilligan's Series Bible For 'Breaking Bad,'"ClickHole. July 27 2015, http://www.clickhole.com/article/vince-gilligans-series-bible-breaking-bad-2836

look at your show. Write the perspective you have of the setting. I love how David Simon, creator of *The Wire*, describes the setting of Baltimore:

> The city is poor; under-educated and struggling with a huge heroin and cocaine problem.[4]

That line above allows me to paint my own picture. *"Cocaine and Heroine" are a part of the setting?* In it, I envision addicts clustered on dirty, poverty stricken streets. Otherwise, who's consuming the drugs? The addicts are a part of the setting. He continues:

> The architecture is of the red-brick and Formstone federal-style rowhouses and townhomes. But in better quadrants of the city there are Victorians and ranchers with lawns and tall oaks. There is a sense that much of the population is gone, fled to the suburbs. Vacant houses seem to outnumber occupied rowhouses in the worst parts of the city.

I love how he smartly classifies the areas by letting us know that quadrants, and therefore classes of people, separate his world. Every word he uses is well thought-out; for example, he describes lawns in the better parts of Baltimore. In other parts of his description of the setting, Simon contrasts the quadrants by giving a sense of what it is like to be poor in the summer versus the winters. He writes, "Winters are cold, summers are hot." For me, it alludes to lack of air conditioning and I get a sense of people just standing out in the heat during the summer, passing time. Likewise, the winters being cold instead of cozy alludes to the lack of all the stuff that makes a place feel warm and fuzzy.

My point is that something is happening in my mind is as I read this. My blank slate is becoming full with imagery. You too want whoever is reading this section of your bible to leave with more than just a blank slate. You want them to see what you see, the way you envision it.

Another cool example of setting and location, is in Vince Galligan's *Breaking Bad* bible:

> In my vision, *Breaking Bad* will be a show that takes place both nowhere and everywhere – the essential idea is that the

---

[4] "The Wire Bible," April 16, 2009, http://kottke.org.s3.amazonaws.com/the-wire/The_Wire_-_Bible.pdf

29

characters live in this nomadic city that wanders where it pleases, never stopping in the same place two nights in a row. To achieve this effect, we will actually construct the entire town, complete with houses and parks, then lash it into the back of an enormous truck bed, ½ mile across by 1 mile long. This truck will always be in motion for each day of shooting, driving all around the US, down into Mexico, and ultimately across the sea to Africa. I know this is a big ask, but I feel it is essential to the show's tone.

A large mistake that most content creators make is not appropriately taking what is in their heads and writing it out descriptively, or even making the mistake of not imaging the setting at all. As embarrassing as it feels to admit that I've made this mistake, I know so many of you reading this have made this very common mistake of not fully imagining the world of your project through your characters' eyes. This is not a recipe for success, and it demonstrates the importance of creating a bible just to be able to fully imagine every trait of the project you are creating.

Character descriptions

You will also need to create a description of each main character that you have scripted. You can describe your characters by adding anything that makes them unique and important to the whole picture using their characteristics, nuances, backstory, secrets and their relationships with others. Your character descriptions should show your attitude towards them because it is, after all, how you want people watching your show or film to feel when watching them. Using Vince Gilligan's bible again, I highlight a simple but well-written character description:

> Walter White – The bald, angry teacher. In the show's universe, teachers are people who have tried to drown cars and must write on chalkboards for the rest of their lives as punishment. Walter spends every day standing in front of a roomful of sleeping children writing chalkboard equations estimating how much sulfuric acid he would need to dissolve a Honda Accord. When the Pink Jester finally visits and offers to make him a villain, Walt says, "Finally…"

In his description (that is not written here), Vince lists what Walt wears, his catch phrase, and other important facts about Walt.

In your character description, you could put anything of importance in it, just don't forget to use your creativity.

*Episode breakdown/Act structure**

Your episode breakdowns should be at least a paragraph and should describe what viewers will expect to see in that episode. When writing your breakdown, think of the storylines: A story, B story, and so on.

Also, write about your show's structure; does it have three, four, or six acts? Will it always begin in a particular location and end in another, or have a tag and/or teaser? If they are self-contained episodes, you could explain what the audience can expect to see in each episode, or if it is a series, how the intensity heightens from episode to episode.

It's important to create a bible so you can fully understand the world of your show or film; you should envision and know every aspect of it. Remember my story about pitching the executive producer, Tracey Baker Simmons, who told me to create a format bible? When I was creating that format, I learned just how little I knew about the structure of my show. There were many elements I hadn't fully visualized. So when it came time for me to answer questions in the bible, I was clueless.

I have had people ask me if a bible is needed if they aren't looking to pitch their project. I answer an unquestionable, yes, because all too often many people don't envision all the aspects of their project. They may understand the concept, but haven't thought about the visual elements of it. How can anyone fully bring to fruition a project that hasn't been completely visualized? What happens is the creativity is left up to the crew and the vision becomes watered down.

You cannot expect that a crew, or anyone you are selling your project to for that matter, will fully imagine what you haven't, even if they are interested in your idea. What will end up happening is they will create a show that they visualize. I can guarantee you what they have in their head is NOT the same thing you have in yours, and when it's all said and done, the show that goes on air or film will be nothing like what you imagined it to be. You have to close your eyes and pen everything you see in your mental imagery about your project. Warning: if you don't pen it, it may be a much harder sell because there may be many things you haven't worked out.

· This relates to televisions shows only.

2) Create a Treatment·

When I was starting out, I confused having a treatment with a long synopsis. Boy was I wrong. What I learned is that filmmakers typically write a treatment before they write the full script and it isn't a short or simple process at all, but it is really effective at carving out the meat of the film, especially for pitching purposes.
Create a detailed outline within your treatment of how your film will look scene by scene; describing what would happen in each scene. After your outline is complete write a detailed description of the plot and how it develops beat by beat. I know you may be thinking, "Well, I may as well write the script!" But your treatment won't be as long as a script – although it can be as long as 15-30 pages.

Plainly put, your treatment should read as a narrative story, written as you visualize it unfolding. It should give examples of dialogue that will take place within the story as well as possible film direction, and it should be written in a way that describes the mood and tone of the film. A great way to prepare to write a treatment is to mind map your idea. Use your mind map to create an outline of potential scenes and categorize your ideas into a succession of scenes. Then close your eyes and visualize each scene, followed by writing a synopsis of what you visualized. Each synopsis should build into a beautifully crafted treatment.

Whether you write the script or not, this treatment can be used to commission a writer or to pitch your idea to a studio house, production company, or network.

3) Create a Format Bible ·

A TV format is a branded show concept created with the possibility of being remade or replicated in other markets around the world. In brief, a format is a type of show that is structured in such a way that it delivers a repetitive experience every time the show is watched so the viewer can know what to expect. It's a tool that is designed to help you be as creative as you can be when creating an original constructed show. The bible is a formatted proposal of an idea that is very visual. The format bible can be for an unscripted or scripted show and is a tool to help you

---

· This relates only to films

· This relates only for shows that are considered a format

protect every element of it. The most common formats are game, competition, and reality show.

When I think of formatted shows, I think of shows like, *The Voice*, *The Bachelor*, *Dance Moms*, *American Idol*, *The Rap Game*, *Bring It*, and *America's Next Top Model*. Most of the shows I mentioned aired or airs in other countries under very similar names, but their copyrighted show structure closely resembles that of the original.

Format bibles are comprised of many of the same parts that make up a pitch and/or show bible. But there is a lot more creativity involving the structure of the show that goes into the format bible. A fully completed format bible will include the following ingredients:

- Title Page – Your title page should give an idea of the atmosphere of the show.
- Table of contents – This is necessary because it will be a more in-depth and detailed bible organizing your show's structure from start to finish.
- Business Proposal – Yes, you should include a business proposal in your format bible. Your proposal should include:
  - ➢ the mission of the company and project
  - ➢ the purpose of the project
  - ➢ your marketing ideas
  - ➢ ROI or return of investment
  - ➢ demographic
  - ➢ overview of the project
  - ➢ synopsis
  - ➢ pictures and bios of important crew and talent
  - ➢ schedule for shooting and running time
  - ➢ locations for filming
- Introduction – Your introduction should give a sense of what the show is about. Think ethos. Why does this show matter to the world at large? It should also detail who the key players are: creators, production company, owner, and even what networks you feel your show is perfect for.
- Format Overview – Your format overview should detail what happens in your show, how, and in what order it happens. This should also include the stakes and selection process. For example, if it's a competition show include challenge rules, ranking, and the elimination process.

- Premise/Description – In a neat sentence or two the premise or description of your format will be the core of what your show is about. It's the basic structure of your story. It may give any necessary backstory and tells where the story is going. For example, the premise of *The Voice*, according to Wikipedia, is "it's a reality singing competition to find unsigned singing talent where both the artists and the judges are in competition against each other."

  Some may disagree, but I like to think that *The Wizard of Oz* is a formatted show. It's a film that has been remade over and over from film to television to the stage. Its made-for-TV format rarely changes despite the medium in which it is shown. The premise of *The Wizard of Oz* could be four characters are lost in an unknown world, seeking to find the one who can help them get what they need most. *The Office* is another scripted format adapted from its original in the UK. Its premise is a show that mocks the typical day and people one would find in a 9-5 setting.

  Last, the show *American Idol* is "an American competition show, a television series according to Wiki, that involves discovering recording artists from unsigned singing talents with the winner determined by the viewer."
- Series Structure – The *American Idol* show is a great example to use. The structure of the show starts with the audition rounds first, then the Hollywood round, Las Vegas round, semi-finals, and finals.
- Duration – How many weeks will the format last, how long is each episode?
- Style Elements – Decor. When you close your eyes, what does the show look like? Red Chairs that swivel around? A judge's table of three people? Or is it set on location on an island?
- Cast Description – Will there be a host? Judges? How many cast members, (you can list prototypes), mentors, guest judges?
- Narrative Progression – How long will the season last? What does each show look like as it progresses over the timespan of the episode?
- Episode Breakdown – The breakdown of your episodes should be at least a paragraph explaining what each episode will be about. The episode should have a title and can also be written as a logline.

- Voting or Jury – Who makes the decisions on who wins from week to week?
- Prizes – What is the prize for the winning contestant?

4) Create a One-Sheet

Regardless if you chose a pitch bible, format bible, or treatment you need to create a one-sheet. Your one-sheet is a straight to the point, short description of your story put all on one page. It is a more condensed and succinct version of your bible. It describes the world of your show, including the tone and feel of it, and it gives information about your characters and how they exist within their relationships. It also gives examples of situations your characters would find themselves in. You can use it to follow along with as you are pitching. Many networks and production companies will ask you for one if they are interested in your project. Make sure you understand the buzzwords and add it into your one-sheet.

Some may argue against ever giving the executive a one-sheet, but in my experience, I have had several people within networks and production companies ask for one; however, I suggest never leaving any materials with the person you are pitching during the meeting. Instead, email the buyer the materials once you return home, if asked. By doing this, you keep control of the conversation. When you send over your one-sheet, you can ask, "When can I expect to hear back from you?" or any questions you may have from your meeting that you forgot to ask or thought of after the meeting. You also have an opportunity to make any last-minute changes based upon what came out of the meeting. So, keeping your materials allows you another chance to connect with the buyer and for you to keep yourself and your project at the forefront of their mind. More detail can be found in Chapter 6.

Below is an example of all the elements that should be included in your one-sheet:

a. Name
b. Title
c. Logline
d. Synopsis.

The synopsis should include: (a) the premise, (b) what the project is about, (c) the environment in which it takes place, (d) main character descriptions, (e) their relationships to each other,

(f) their conflicts and character arcs, (g) a description of the themes, (h) genre, (i) and demographic, (j) a description of the mood, tone, and visual, (k) and if it is for TV, you should incorporate episode breakdowns and story arcs all creatively told.

5) Write the Pilot and Film

Everyone who pitches show or film ideas may not intend to write the scripts and that's okay. Some people are great at creating worlds and not scripts. There is no mark against you if you decide not to write for your project. You can go in prepared to say, "We will need to hire writers, I will not be a writer." However, if you are preparing to write the script, you want to make sure you have written a few drafts of the script before you go in to pitch them. You don't want to have an amazing pitch while the script is only subpar.

I once reached out to writer Gina Prince-Bythewood to commend her on her film *Beyond the Lights*, and she informed me that it took her 55 drafts to get it right. I'm not saying you need to do 55 drafts of your scripts, but you should be prepared to hand over your best work – after all, first impressions are the best impressions and you want to be able to hook them from their first read.

If you are writing the script, do it *before* you reach out to pitch. I can't tell you how many drafts you should do before your script is at a good enough place to hand over, but it should be polished. I spoke with independent filmmaker Nathan Adloff (*Miles*), who said his script was only half completed when an executive producer asked to read it and offered to come on board with the project. I surmise that the writing had to be damn good for him to say, "Yes, I will help you." Somewhere, somehow, that executive producer connected with it. If you aren't a great writer, maybe you can commission a great writer to come on board and help you co-write your script.

6) Package Your Project

Packaging is attaching talent, producers, a director or writer to your projects. Let's say you have a really great idea and are about to pitch it to the network of your choice. Now imagine a production company is coming in to the same network to pitch their project which is really similar to yours. Now further imagine them saying that they have locked in actresses Queen Latifah and Katie Holms; director Tom Verica (*Scandal*, *How to Get Away With Murder*); and executive producer

David Hollander. Both projects are what the network is looking for. Both projects are developed greatly and have pretty good scripts already written. The only difference is one has attachments and one doesn't. Which do you think the network will choose?

Underrepresented, independent content creators often find themselves without a sales agent to help them package their projects and so are left to do the tricky job themselves. With or without an agent to help you, packaging is a must. And just like pitching to networks and investors, it takes a bit of research and craftsmanship, but I'm sure you can do it. The more you package your project, especially if it is good, the more likely you are to beat out the competition.

Let's face it: someday you will more than likely have a similar project to someone else. The more packaged your project, the better chance it will have and the more control you will have. Networks don't want to do the work for you to package your projects. That's why they suggest you team up with a production company first, so they don't have to labor on your project. This doesn't mean you have to have every role filled. You only need as few as one to two people attached to the project, but the more the merrier. The point is you want to bring something to the table other than your creativity, which could be anyone from actors to directors, writers, investors or EPs.

Okay, so you have a great screenplay. Your goal is to take it to all of the major film festivals and to get a distribution deal. Or you have a teleplay or unscripted television show with a goal to get the show optioned, or monies invested to shoot the pilot with hopes of it getting picked up for series, but you have no clue how to make these goals happen. You don't have representation, so how will you get in the doors to pitch to people who can take the show to the next level? You probably didn't think to reach out to a packaging agent who can help package your film or television project with talented and well-known talent, writers, directors, and investors. No, that's not the direction you thought to take. And even if you had considered a packaging agent, you would have to pitch them, and they would then have to consider if your project is worth taking on.

When I started pitching, I didn't know what a packaging agent was or that I could get one as an independent content creator. In fact, one of my biggest mistakes early on in pitching was that though I had great ideas, I didn't offer anything else beyond the idea. I believe I had pitched at least ten to fifteen times before I ever considered packaging the project.

I thought all I needed was an idea. I look back and realize that had I packaged my projects it could have helped to take them much further than they had gone, if not all the way. If you learn from this mistake you can easily fall into the 80-90% percentile of successful pitches. As a content creator, you should package your projects and have more to offer when you come to the table.

Like me, you may be just as clueless about the process of packaging a project as I was. In most cases, if you are independent, you are packaging your project all on your own and seeking out-of-the-box ways to pitch your projects to the various people who could make it a success. The suggestions I give are ones that have worked for many independent content creators I have spoken with like yourselves and suggestions given to me through the interviews I have had with development executives and producers.

So how do you package your project?

It's a question that I'm often asked and an issue I'm constantly faced with. As an independent content creator, I mean when you are really independent, you are almost forced to wear a lot of freaking hats! Which means even after you've written the script, you have to be very creative if you are planning to create a film or television show that will ultimately get a distribution deal.

When I first began pitching, I thought it was all about having a great idea and at the most, writing a great script. But, I soon learned that even if you have a great idea, and/or have written a great script, you need to attach not only *talented* people to carry your idea to fruition, but you need *recognizable* people as well. And there is a difference between the two.

When casting for the first short film I ever produced, my partner and I first sought semi-professional actors, and up-and-coming talent, but we struggled with who would play the antagonist of the film. The role, very important to the themes of the film, was probably more important than the protagonist's role in my opinion, as it was a very emotionally driven role that had very few lines. Three of our top choices at the time were: Hisham Tawfiq, (before his series regular role on the *Blacklist*), Nashawn Kearse, and Tobias Truvillion. All at that time had promising acting careers. I can't remember what happened, except that Hisham Tawfiq politely declined the offer. To our novice credit, as this was both of our first time making a film, we went after the very talented, Michael K. Williams (*Boardwalk Empire*). We reached out to his manager who asked for the script to read. After some time, his manager reached back out to us saying that Michael really liked the script, but wasn't available for the shooting of the film due to his schedule with *Boardwalk Empire*. Our search continued and we landed on the very skilled Shiek Mahmud-Bey to play the role.

Likewise, we searched for a team to help carry out our film as we envisioned. We searched a couple of months for a director and cinematographer. We found a couple of great and talented people whose work to this day I still admire. The talent we cast were skilled and some even recognizable enough to take the film much further than we had expected. Especially considering that the life span of short films is very…short. In fact, that film, the first I produced, to date, has been displayed in millions of households within in the US. Yet, I have learned over the years that in order for your project to have legs to run with, you need to bring to the table *recognizable* names. Had our film been a feature film or television show without recognizable talent, it probably would not have been a picked up by a network.

I learned over time that talented and skillful are completely different and miles apart from recognizable. Skillful and talented attachments may be good for your project, but recognizable attachments help get deals and network attention. Many times a distribution company, network, and investor will ask, "Who's attached?" To say, "Well, I have very seasoned, veteran actors," does not weigh much and will not necessarily make them inquire further about your project. As an actress, I am skillful and very talented, but I am unsure I would be able to get a network or investor to sign on the dotted line. Executives are thinking dollars and cents and aren't thinking about one without the other – they want skilled, talented, *and well known*. So you definitely want to work hard in this area to attach recognizable talent to your project so that you can grab the attention of the buyers you are pitching. In the words of indie film producer, Tanya Thompson, (*The 1 Closest 2 U, Where the Heart Lies, The Hills*):

> If you are in independent film making, even celebrities are doing independent films, you are competing with people who have bigger budgets and names, so you want to make sure your production value is there. If you can get at least one to two names you should. I would encourage anybody to save as much

money as they could to put names into your films. If you have names, you are probably going to get a distribution deal. Even if the production value isn't as good, you are probably going to get a distribution deal.

If you only can get one, you are good, if you get two you are golden, if you get three, hands down you are good to go! They want names. That's what these distribution companies want. It's important if you want to sell your film and get it to a bigger platform. Those are the two things that almost every distribution company told me; production value and names."

You may ask *"How do I attach well-known talent to my project if I don't have an agent?"* Consider the suggestions below.

Create your wish list

Have you created a wish list of people you want to work with yet? If not, stop reading right now and create a list of people who could take your project to the next level. The list can include: actors, producers, writers, directors, investors, DPs, and whoever else recognizable you can think of.

Use your social media connection

Start now building the relationships you are interested in attaching to your project. No seriously, stop reading and at least see if you can connect with them via social media. LinkedIn has become my friend! I have made many connections via LinkedIn, especially network executives and investors. Now that you have your list start connecting with them on social media. See where they are most active.

Ask for a soft introduction

It was once said to me that we all have in our networks at least 200 people; though you may not be best friends with them all, you have a minimum of 200 people in your network. If you do the math, that means you have at least 40,000 people in your network. For me, this means that someone I know knows someone I need to know to take my project to the next level. Just knowing that you know someone who knows someone should take the pressure of packaging off of you. Think of it this way, the people you need to attach to your project are simply an ask or two away. You've created your wish list, now it's time to use your network.

Imagine you are at a film premiere event one night and are talking to the host of the event who happens to be someone you have worked with in the past on another project. He mentions that he has just finished the final draft of his script and that Queen Latifah is now attached to his project. It just so happens that you too have a project where she is at the top of your wish list. What do you do next? You ask a huge favor is what you do. If not in that moment, you want to ask him later if he wouldn't mind doing a soft introduction to her so that you can ask her to read your script.

I ask a lot nowadays! I have asked people for soft introductions to network executives and I have introduced other *trustworthy* content creators who have asked me to introduce them to network executives. I have even written out the message for them to pass along to the person I am seeking to pitch. This way, they didn't have to struggle with writing up something amazing about my project or me. I just did it myself and put it in third person.

Notice the highlighted word trustworthy? I want to be clear that not just anyone can come to me asking me to introduce them to people I know. Also, I mostly asked people who knew me, my business ethics, and/or someone I was presently establishing a relationship with. If I was presently establishing a relationship with them, then my ask would be, "If you find while getting to know me that you can trust me, my creative genius, and my work ethic, feel free to introduce me to anyone who could help me with my bottom line..." or something like that.

I have known people who push the limits on the relationships they have established, and in my opinion, their handling of certain relationships was borderline abusive or plain annoying. By that I mean, they followed up too quickly or reached out too much. When asking big favors, you have to treat that newfound relationship as if it is extremely fragile; always put yourself on the other end and ask, "How would I take this or that," or "How would this land with me?" You don't want to destroy the relationship with the person who introduced you by harassing the person they introduced you to or that person may never introduce you to anyone again.

I have a friend and colleague, Sybil Amuti, who is a proven success in marketing and branding. She suggested that I connect with all of the people on my wish list and then connect with all of the people at their companies or in their networks, even down to the administrative assistant. Never, ever, underestimate the power of the executive assistant or the coordinator; they hold the keys to your success. They are the gatekeepers and if you have favor with them, you win.

My marketing friend also suggested that after connecting with all the people, create articles and posts that grab their attention. This way they can begin to trust you as an expert in the field and you can begin to build on the relationship. When you finally ask for a meeting to pitch them or attach them to your project, they already feel they can trust your work.

Contact the talent's manager

One way to get talent to look at your project is to go through their manager. I purposely didn't say an agent because I believe it may not be the best first step to take. While there are many loving agents in the world, their job is simply to employ the talent and make money for themselves. A manager's job is to help shape their clients' careers and guide each client step-by-step in getting exposure. A manager may better understand the heart of the talent more than the agent. Also, manager's work closely with the talent so is more apt to know what projects are better suited for their clients than an agent. Reach out to the managers of the prospective talent and appeal to them to read your script.

To put this theory to the test, first, I asked a casting director friend of mine if she could connect me to a well-known and recognizable actor with whom she was a friend. She was nice enough to connect me to the actor. The actor hadn't responded to my request initially. I decided to follow up with his manager. It was a smoother sailing process from that point on. The manager, who responded less than an hour later, asked many questions to make sure what I was asking was right for his client and in alignment with his client's goals. Though the actor never signed on to work with me due to timing, the process was pretty simple and the system worked. I definitely recommend going this route.

Partner with a casting director

You may consider partnering with a casting director to package your project. According to casting guru, Tracey "Twinkie" Byrd (*Southside With You, Notorious, Being Mary Jane, Fruitvale Station*), "A skilled casting director will be able to align the goals you have set for your project with the right cast, whether its for distribution purposes, film festivals, acquisitions or to reach as many people as possible." A casting director can add much value to your project because of their rolodex of

42

talent they have. Casting directors are experts at creating character breakdowns that will attract the right talent, and because they know an array of talent, they are able to think outside of the box for casting.

A casting director has relationships with actors as well as producers, writers, and directors and if he or she is seeking to expand their resumes with a producer credit, they may actually call in a few favors from "named" talent. Content creators may think, *"Well, I don't have the money to pay a casting director,"* But I wouldn't let that stop you from asking them for their help. Just make sure to give them a comparable offer in return.

A documentary short film I co-wrote and directed was an official selection of the Golden Door Film Festival. I attended a workshop of a casting director who happened to also have a film she produced in the festival. I knew the casting director well. She had cast me in several projects before, but I hadn't known that she was also a producer. While sitting in her workshop, she expressed why she decided to partner with the filmmakers and cast their show. It was there that I realized many casting directors have other goals of filmmaking and maybe their career has landed them in casting.

I was also asked to present an award to a casting director at the Ocktober Film Festival of New York. I had asked the casting director for her bio because I needed it to prepare my speech to honor her. As I read her bio, I learned that she initially moved to New York to become a director and filmmaker and that her career led her to casting. Knowing this, I would approach the casting director and ask if he/she would be interested in casting and producing or directing a web-series. The goal is to make the offer extremely appealing.

What to do if you can't package it on your own

If you are unlucky at packaging on your own, or you don't feel confident in doing the job, you should begin pitching production companies first. A network doesn't have the time to package your projects, but production companies will take the time to further develop your project if they like it. A production company will help you package, shoot your sizzle reel, and sell the show to a network. This goes without saying, but I'm going to say it anyway: reach out to the production companies that have relationships with the network or studios that are on your wish list.

I understand that most independent content creators are really seeking to get their stories told, but I also feel we should be very intentional in our process and build a strategy that works for us in the long run and not just for the moment. Taking some time to attach the right people to your project will work greatly in your favor. Think of it this way, would you view a film by a filmmaker unheard of? With unknown talent featured on the cover art? With an unknown director? Put in a different way, what is it that makes you tune into a television show? Go view a film? Click play on Netflix or Hulu? What is it that grabs your attention? It's not to say that the themes of your project won't grab the attention of those seeking to be entertained, but you must be honest with yourself that the reason you tune in to watch most shows or films is someone recognizable is attached to the project.

7) Create a Look Book

It was Nathan Adloff, an independent filmmaker and creator of the movie *Miles* (Molly Shannon, Paul Reiser, Missi Pyles), who first introduced me to the harsh reality that I was pitching potential investors the wrong way! I cringe when I think about not having a look book to pass along to investors, but I appreciate the moment of growth.

A look book is a graphic-designed presentation that strongly conveys your project in a way that is visually enticing, explaining what your project will look and feel like. The look book is not only designed as a tool for pre-production so that everyone can be on the same page, it is created so that people who aren't experienced in film or television can understand the visual concept of your creation.

Your look book should include:

- Pictures of named or celebrity talent you have attached, the role they play in your project, and their bios
- Pictures of key players like casting directors, writers, directors, producers, and executive producers, their bios and pictures of the work they've already done
- Your concept and/or logline, synopsis, tone, directors and or producer's statement
- Insight into the characters in the film by including pictures of characters in other films that are similar.
- Information on the visual strategy of the film with pictures that communicate your ideas

- Pictures or location references
- The financing structure and sales projections so that investors can get an idea of the return on their investment should they invest

Your look book should come as close as possible to the look and feel that a sizzle reel would, only with the financial aspect of your production added. The person or team reading your look book should gain a good understanding of the film you will be creating, so you want to make sure it resembles what you see when you close your eyes. You can start working on this book after you have done all of the groundwork listed in earlier chapters. You can then get a line producer to start working through the numbers portion of the look book.

8) Enlist a Script Coverage Service

If you have a show or film you are working on and have written a script, the first thing you should do is make sure it's at its best. I suggest having your script evaluated by an analyst through a script coverage service. Script coverage is an analytical report that's written on your script and then given a grade. Whether you are pitching a network, production company or studio, someone in development will most likely analyze your script (maybe an assistant or coordinator) to decide if the script should be either passed on or considered further. It is best to have your scripts analyzed before pitching anyone to make sure it is in its best form, especially before sending your script to a development team. You will receive a comprehensive review of your script with notes on the logline and synopsis, overview, and/or treatment. Your script will also be graded based on these criterions: plot, character development, structure, and dialogue. Script coverage is a great way to see how your script translates to your viewer and how you can improve your script. For good coverage ranging between $100-$350 (depending on what company you use), it is more than worth it to be able to feel confident about your script when pitching.

Pitching Challenge #2

Today you are at a speed dating pitch fest and have a short amount of time to sell your project to the buyer. Buyer #1 sits in the seat across from you.

1. First, pick a potential buyer (network, studio house, production company, investor, or talent).

2. What is the first thing you will do when you sit down?
3. What are the first three things you will mention about your project? List them in the order you will say/pitch them.
4. Last, what do you know about the potential buyer? Any commonalities between them and your project? Incorporate anything you know about them, their company, or network into your pitch.
5. Put five minutes on a timer and practice the pitch you just wrote out.

Go…

Follow-up questions:

1. How do you feel about the results of your pitch?

2. Any discoveries?

3. What parts of your pitch do you want to keep?

4. What parts of your pitch need work?

Now go back and listen to pitch #1. How did you grow? Write out your successes and the things you'd like to keep from this pitch.

CHAPTER FOUR

Preparing the Pitch

My idea of hell is God showing me everything
I could have accomplished, if only I tried.
—Wes Moore's Sister

You've developed the world of your show, you have written the pilot or film script, or collaborated with a writer to write it. What should you do next?
CELEBRATE!

No, seriously, you should take a moment to celebrate every small success. Do you know how awesome it is that you completed the creation of a television show or film? Not many people can say the same thing. Far too often we are so busy looking to make the big picture happen that we overlook all of our small successes – like writing a script...a whole script! That takes a lot of creative genius. So, celebrate now because after the celebration you have a lot of work to do.

Pitch #38 - Robert Townsend: TELL ME THE STORY!

One of the most important lessons I learned about pitching came from a meeting a co-writer and I had with Robert Townsend. He was doing some behind the scenes in Miami for a project he was working on and we were there too, all of us attending the American Black Film Festival. We had three pitch meetings set for that week and his was the second pitch meeting. Our first, with Aspire TV's general manager Paul Butler, had gone well. At least we had made a connection with him and his team, and they liked our project, but they weren't ready for one of its magnitude at the time.

Initially, Robert declined meeting with us. "No, he doesn't have time," his assistant wrote back to me after reaching out to ask her for a meeting. But the day before our flight to Miami, I received an email from her saying that Robert would like to meet with us after all. She informed us that if interested, we would pitch him on camera as he was working on a project. Those were his conditions. We weren't necessarily thrilled about the set-up, but we relented because we wanted to get in front of him, "Oh...okay, sure. We'll take the meeting."

Once we settled in at the location with Mr. Townsend, his camera crew was all set up and ready to go. We sat down at the table. With cameras positioned, we started going through our PowerPoint pitch deck that was on my MacBook. Bullet by bullet we went through the deck, then a quarter of the way through, he stopped us. "Wait, wait, wait, wait! What are you doing? What are you looking at?" We were a little confused. Overall, this was our third time pitching this TV show idea, and never before had we been so abruptly interrupted. I said, "We are looking at our pitch deck." Aggressively, he said, "Just tell me the story. Like, just tell me the story. It should be in your heart," he said along with some other stuff that I cannot even remember.

Almost instantly, I became offended by his reaction. I shut down. I felt I was going to say the wrong thing to him in retaliation from being offended. Looking back, this was probably one of the worst pitching moments I'd ever had, and at the same time, one of the best teaching moments ever. My writing partner continued telling the story. After a few minutes had passed, I joined in again. We spoke passionately from our hearts. We discussed the storylines and themes in the episodes; we talked about our character arcs and their flaws from a place of genuine passion. Once we finished, Mr. Townsend blurted, "That's what I'm saying! Finally! Okay, that is a great story. Now, that's something I would buy in to."

He asked more questions about locations, setting, and characters, and we filled him in on all of the details. Then he said, "It's too big. It's too much. It's your first show. You guys need to cut this down. There are too many moving parts." Our meeting carried on in this fashion for another 30 minutes or so. Shut down. Build up. It felt that way to me.

We finished the pitch. We shook hands…for his camera crew. But once the cameras were off, I said to Robert Townsend, "You know I hate you, right? Like I literally, wanted to slap you. You know that, right?" He looked at me, astonished at how frank I was, and he burst out laughing. His laughter made us laugh…a little. (Don't worry…I have a way of telling the truth through laughter so as not to offend, even though my feelings were 99.9% real. I also sent a thank you email thanking him for his knowledge; happy he had a sense of humor.) Robert Townsend expressed no further interest in our pitch.

Plainly put, he was right. I would find it to be a repeated lesson over the course of my next few pitches. I had to learn how to tell my story from the heart. We knew our story. We'd spent months creating it. It was in our hearts. We just didn't trust ourselves enough. It's a lesson I will spend my life teaching others. Trust that you know your story.

Practice, Practice, Practice

If I have learned anything over my years of pitching, I have learned the best way to perfect it is by doing it. This chapter is all about practicing and perfecting your pitch. By now, you know the best way to pitch is by telling a story. You may have spent a lot of time writing your story and then building it into great pitching materials, and now it is time to practice your pitch. Throughout this chapter, I will give lessons to make sure that you are putting into practice what you have learned so you can master your pitch!

The goal of this chapter is to come up with ways to best sell your project to anyone. The objective is to help you piece together the most compelling parts of your story and suggest some ways of pitching you may not have considered.

The Rules:

You must practice. This works if you work it. Please do not simply read the chapter without putting the book down and doing the work. Do not come up with excuses why you cannot do it *now*. Even if you have not fully developed the concept yet, you should still do the practice. Practicing it will also bring forth all the loopholes in the development of your concept. You can always, and you should, come back to this practice and do it repeatedly. In fact, I suggest you use the exercises before each pitch meeting you have. If you do these practices, you will find new and exciting discoveries about your project and new ways of pitching them.

To be clear, pitching is a subjective undertaking. Because of this, every person applying these methods will walk away with a different pitch; one's pitch is decided by his or her project, experiences, and personality. There is no one format in which one should pitch, but there are some best practices that you could use to help you build out a pitch that is perfect for you. We will spend time in the chapter piecing together ways in which you can best tell your story. However, you will be the ultimate decision maker on what you choose to do once you get into the room or on the phone – even an elevator. This chapter will help you tap into what the most important parts of your story are and how to sell it.

The Pitch: Where and How to Start

I am asked all of the time, and am sure now, that the biggest uncertainty for content creators learning to pitch is knowing how to begin the pitch, then what to say. I have witnessed content creators ramble on and on and sing praises about their story idea, beginning with things like, "You're going to love this story," or "My main character will touch the hearts of many," and much more of this hyperbole before ever telling the story.

I once coached a person whose passion about his project was so endearing that it would certainly lure the receiver into wanting to hear more. Then at the end of his pitch, having never shared any plot points, characteristics, important themes, or much of anything that made up the story and its greatness, I said, "But...what is the story? I hear your passion, but can you send me a one-sheet or the script, because I really do not know any more about the story now that you have pitched it."

Are you guilty of this? If you are doing this in your pitch meetings, I want to persuade you to stop all meetings right now. In this man's case and probably yours too, you have not fully developed your project. This guy had all of the ideas in his head, but hadn't written much of it down on paper. His thoughts came across jumbled and his pitch was all over the place and unorganized. The best advice I could give him after listening to him pitch several times was to stop and fully put on paper what was in his head because he was potentially losing out on opportunities to take his project to the next level by being unprepared.

If you find yourself pitching how great the success of your script will be and never tell the plot points of your story, know that many of the people who listen to pitches all the time will recognize your lack of preparation right off the bat. Using hyperbole is a dead giveaway that you are unprepared.

Having said that, the strategy and practice steps that follow will help you get to the true nuts and bolts of what your story is about much quicker so that you can utilize your time in the room effectively and even get to other points about your project that could help you make the sell.

The guy above isn't alone, I coach quite a few people and watch them all make the same mistake, a mistake I once made pitching. Without knowing where they should start in their pitch, the content creator nervously starts reading from their paper: the logline first, then continues reading the synopsis and reading on from there. Are you guilty of this? Not to worry, you are not alone.

At first, many people suck at pitching. Pitching is certainly not as easy as it sounds. It's a craft that only gets better with knowledge and practice.

51

In fact, every time I'm pitching a new project, I probably suck at it at first. Practicing it helps me to work through my thoughts. The impromptu pitching helps me to gain clarity on what's really important about my project. So, like Mr. Robert Townsend once instructed me to, "just tell the story," I will give you the same instruction...

Pitching Challenge #3

Put down the book and just talk about your project from your heart. What is it about?

STOP. Try doing this. There aren't any rules. I just want you to talk through what your story is about. Place three minutes on the timer again and practice using your notes.

GO...

At this point, like me, most content creators are able to tell a more compelling story. If you have done the work, have fully constructed the film's complete beginning, middle and end, or developed your show's concept and format and all its elements, you naturally will begin telling a story about your project starting with the most captivating parts of it.

Follow-up questions:

1. Did your storytelling get better?

2. In telling your story, did you use the same things from earlier practices, or did you talk about something else? Write out all of the newer points you made in your pitch practice.

3. What still needs work?

4. If you had to make any changes, what would they be?

When you are pitching, you must trust that the time you have spent creating the world of your project and characters is engrained in your heart. When it is time to pitch your idea, you do not want to hide behind a computer or pitch deck. You want your passion to radiate while you are telling the best story you can tell. Trust that you know the project in your heart. In fact, if you decide to use a pitch deck (which is pretty much a Power Point presentation) as your paper pitch, just put the topics on it you want to cover and let them guide you through your story while leaving out all the details. In essence, you only need a bulleted agenda to look at while you pitch your project.

If you want, try doing that: put the important topics that make up your project down on paper (topics only), and use it to guide you through your next pitching practice.

Try pitching it again. This time write out an updated list of topics you want to cover in your pitch based on the previous pitches you have done. Use them as your guide. Trust that the details of the story are in your heart. Put time on the clock.

Go…

Still Don't Know Where to Start Your Pitch?

Every time I pitch, I ask myself "where do I start?" I'm sure it's a question that plagues most people. How do you compress a two-hour story, or one that spans 10–11 weeks into a five-minute pitch? In short, the answer is to start with the story.

In order to answer the burning question, "where to start my pitch," let's discuss the important elements that make an effective pitch no matter if it's television, digital, or film content you are pitching.

They are:

Title
Genre
Concept (can be logline)
Premise
Characters/prototypes
Plot/Story/Description/Overview
Setting/Location/Backdrop
Structure/Style Elements/Show Run-through
Story Arc/Climax/Episodes
Character Arc
Themes
Hook

I believe no matter what type of concept you are pitching, the elements above should be included. Knowing how to combine these elements into your pitch will help to ensure all of the buyer's essential questions are

53

answered. Mix it with other unique concept features while you are pitching and it will make your pitch come to life. The art of pitching is in highlighting your concept's originality. The uniqueness of your pitch could come in any form: in the unlikely characters you have attached, in the character's journey, the way you tell the story, or on your personal experiences applied to a common situation. While the saying, "There are no new stories," may have *some* validity, what you have to determine is what about your "unoriginal" story is unique and original. You have to know your story's hook. The hook of your story is in its distinctiveness. You should be able to pitch what makes your story different from the ones that are seemingly like it. The magic of pitching lies in the uniqueness and originality of that small difference. Ron Simmons, of SimonSays Entertainment, said it best, "There are no new stories, but the lens in which they are told is what is intriguing."

Many new pitchers will usually start with the logline of their project. How many of you used the logline in your pitch above? How many of you read from the paper? It is okay; your minds will open up to other ideas after reading this book. Using a logline in your pitch could work, provided the logline is killer!

A more promising start, that may even be fail proof, is to begin with the premise of your story. Remember, the premise is what happens initially in your story that drives the plot. What if you were pitching and you started telling the story at the part that sets things in action? If you start with the situation that sends your main character on his journey, then I believe you cannot go wrong. To get started, one question you may consider asking yourself when preparing your pitch is, *"What has happened to set my story into action? What is driving the plot?"* If I were to pitch starting with the premise of a film, an example would be:

"Tiny is about a boy who mistakenly drinks a potion that makes him microscopic..."

Or in greater detail:

> At school, Tiny Stuart is a socially awkward nerd and is always either being taken advantage of by the jocks and/or used by the "it" girls of the schools. One day in Science class he frustratingly mistakes a tube of shriveling potion with his soft drink and gulps it down turning himself into a minuscule-sized human that no one can see with the human eye.

54

In the above examples, I state the title of my project and the premise in one, and I name the main character, give a few characteristics of him, and then state the premise in the other. Both examples are a brief synopsis of what sets the story into play.

Like I wrote earlier, how you begin your pitch will be entirely up to you. However, for practice, begin your pitch with the premise. Let's do another pitching exercise and try a few ways to see if you can begin to piece together a structure for your pitch using the premise as a starting place.

Pitching Challenge #4

Imagine you are at a speed dating pitch fest and a buyer sits across from you. The timer goes off and you now have three minutes to pitch your project. Which way would you choose to pitch if given the choices below?

DO THESE: Scribe your pitch below for each option and practice pitching each way before making a choice.

a. Your name, the title, the premise, then…

- Talk about the journey of the main character
- Discuss the plot points starting from the beginning and going to the middle
- Introduce the conflict and
- Talk through the climatic moments of your project

b. Your name, the title, the premise, then…
- Genre
- Location
- The main characters
- Plot Points

c. Your name, your bio, the title, the premise, then…
- Intriguing question to make them think about the themes
- The main characters
- Plot points
- Themes

d. Your name, the title, the premise then,
   • Genre
   • Discuss the plot points
   • The main characters
   • The character arcs

Which way worked best for you? Did one way seem to flow better than others?

I kept this challenge in mind when trying to answer where to start my pitch in a pitch meeting with Magilla Entertainment. The show I was pitching was about mental illness, a very dark place in the lives of others. I didn't want the room to be sullen during my pitch even though I was talking about mental challenges, so I had to be crafty on the delivery of my pitch. For this pitch it was important to reverse engineer my story because I know it is hard to sell sadness. I started with an upbeat part of my story; the part that I wanted to see happen at the end of each episode, which is healing and happiness. That is where I started my pitch and that is where I ended it. In the middle of my pitch, where I talked about the premise and told the story of each character and their challenging lives, was where I kept the grim parts. Then I built my pitch out from there.

The Three Most Common Ways to Pitch

While these are not the only ways to pitch your idea, these are the three ways that are most common.

The paper pitch

No matter what I always prepare a Power Point presentation deck for all of my pitch meetings. It's really just a way to organize your thoughts and pitch based on the way you want to deliver it. When I first began pitching, I would go through each slide and use it as a visual aid and to guide my talking points. If you choose to pitch this way, (slide by slide), then your slides should be designed to tell a story, each one moving the story along from the beginning to the arc and then to the end. The slides need to have a font big enough that it can be read easily and not have too much information to read. You don't want the buyer to get caught up reading your slide during your pitch – definitely a mistake I made in my past.

As you pitch, you should be building into your story, if applicable, the location, mood, tone, and character descriptions. You can also include other notable selling points into the pitch, but your primary focus should be to tell a compelling story. You can also pitch from a one-sheet, which you can place slightly in front of you to help guide the talking points of your pitch.

Skype interviews

Many use Skype interviews to put their talent on tape. This is done a lot for reality shows as most of the time creators are trying to sell personalities. I like the idea of Skype interviews because you don't have to spend money for the buyer to see the winning personalities of your cast, and it lets them know that you really have attached the people you claim to have attached. You can pull Skype interviews and show the personalities of the people you have on board. This especially works for reality shows! The interviews can be simple guided interviews of you asking your talent questions that they'd find themselves in while on the show. The goal is to showcase your talent, as interesting people an audience would want to sit on their sofas and follow week to week.

Sizzle reel

A sizzle reel is a video, usually around one–five minutes, which sells the highlights of your story. Think of it as a trailer for a movie or highlights for a television premiere. You can produce a sizzle with a few scenes from your project that give an overall understanding of what your project is about.

But let's say you don't have the money to shoot a bunch of scenes to produce an amazing-looking sizzle reel; another suggestion is to rip clips from other shows that have already been done that give off the mood or tone of your show. Consider creating title cards along with the clips and even a voice over to tell your story, as long as you do it in such a way that it moves the story along. If nothing else, you can get your idea out and the sizzle can be used to pitch up the chain.

Of the three, a sizzle reel is probably the most effective pitching material you can use. Creating a well-produced sizzle reel leaves the executives no room to guess what your project is about. They will see exactly what you have in mind.

Tailor Your Pitch

I'm often asked, *"To whom should I pitch my television show or film idea?"*

My advice on deciding where and to whom you should pitch your idea is to do a mind map. First, if you haven't already done this, you want to get to the core of what your show is about so that you can get it into the home of your most perfect viewer.

To establish the ideal audience you first should know the themes of your show and for whom you have created it. Clarity is key here. Ask yourself, what is my show about? Narrow down your demographic. Is it reality driven or docu-styled? Is it about adventure or forgiveness? Is it a show for hopeless romantics or troubled women? DIY'ers, guy-humor? For 18-24-year-olds or 35-44-year-olds? The more info you can dump into your map the better.

It's similar to the car commercial where the man says, "I want a car," and every car known to man fills the television screen. Then he says, "A red car," and immediately all of the other cars that aren't red exit the screen. Then he becomes more and more concrete, leaving him with the car of his dreams. Your mind map should do the same for you. The more you come up with about your show, the narrower the focus and the network possibilities become.

After you've done this, you can create a wish list based on the networks that share the same demographics and themes from the list you created above.

The next few questions to answer are: what shows on air are similar in topic and demographics to mine and what networks are they on? Similarly, you can do the same for your films. Which production companies or studios have distributed, produced, or put out films like mine? When packaging your projects, ask what executive producers have produced comparable shows. It may take a little research on your end to come up with a comprehensive list for each of the categories above, but it's worth it. You certainly don't want to go to a network or production company and pitch a fast, action driven, and crime-fighting show if they are known for doing female dramas. You are wasting everyone's time and doing yourself and possibly your career a tremendous disservice! The development team that gave you the opportunity to be heard will now consider you a person who didn't do their homework. So, to avoid this career pitching disaster, do yourself a favor and start with a mind map.

Research Your Subject

Before you can begin your mind map, you should first research the person or company you are pitching. Don't simply look at what's on Wikipedia or on their site for information. There is a lot of other information available to you on the web that can help you gain insight and better understand who you are pitching and how to appeal to them within your pitch.

A great example of this happened on a call with a coaching client about his space opera project. As we were brainstorming who to pitch his project to, I suggested pitching a couple of Viacom's networks. These networks were not on his wish list of networks to pitch. But, I always like to think outside of the box. You never know what direction a network is going in and I saw an area of opportunity. For the last couple of years, Viacom has suffered greatly and news recently traveled that Sumner Redstone, part owner of Viacom, had exiled the now former CEO, Philippe Dauman. My suggestion to my client was to be open-minded and consider adding two of the Viacom networks to his list. I figured with all of the financial trouble Viacom had been having, especially with MTV losing half of its viewership, they were most likely seeking a breakthrough show that could potentially bring it up from troubled waters.

My suggestion was to pitch his space show "as is" without making any changes, but also brainstorm ways and be ready to pitch how he could make it fit the demographics of the two networks I suggested. My reasoning was I felt MTV's demographic, which was a much younger one than my client had intended for his show, could fall in love with his space opera series and potentially create a new space opera trend. I figured he could do what the creators of *SpongeBob SquarePants* did with changing their adult themed show to a kid friendly show. With the trouble MTV is having, they just may be attracted to his show's concept.

My second suggestion was pitching it to Teen Nick. I thought it could fit into the teen space and have the same affects on teens as the vampire phenomenon, *Twilight* had. My knowledge of Viacom's troubled networks and current shows allowed me to think outside of the box during our brain dump for the pitching wish list for his show. He and I brainstormed and strategized ways to make his show work for the two networks. In our brainstorm and research he remained open to all options, though he went with his initial ideas for his show.

Here are questions for research that will allow you to appeal to the heart of the person or company you are pitching to:

- Has the network, production company or studio, actor, executive producer, director, or writer done similar projects to yours?
- Have they not done any similar projects? This may work in your favor too. Maybe they, especially actors, are seeking a project that is similar to yours they can sink their teeth into.
- Has an actor stated he/she would like to work on independent projects for films with subject matter that isn't commercialized?
- What are the mission statements of the company?
- What actors mentioned in articles or on talk shows they want to try other types of roles that specifically align with your show?
- There are lulls in actors, directors, or writers' careers. Are they seeking an opportunity to work on a great project to get noticed again?
- Based on their philanthropic work, what specific interests do potential investors have?

Additionally,

- Read all the latest articles of networks to see if they speak about different directions their company is going in.
- Read all the trades to remain in the know.
- Learn about hobbies to see if any correlates to your project.
- Search to see if anyone on your lists is passionate about social issues.
- Check social media and articles to see if anyone on your list has a passion for the themes of your project.

While the above bulleted list is only a few research suggestions, there are multitudes of other things you can research to find similarities between you and the person or company whose heart you will soon persuade.

As a reminder, remember that content creators should remain flexible with our projects, as I'm sure animator Stephen Hillenburg had to be when he turned his adult themed show, *SpongeBob,* into one for children. It doesn't mean that you lose your original vision, or that the vision has to change entirely, it just means you have to flex your creative abilities and add addendums to the idea.

Activating your creativity will work in your favor because each network you pitch your idea to has a different audience of viewers they must appease, and your flexibility lends to the probability of your show getting on air.

Mind Map Your Pitch

Once you've completed your research and your wish list, you are ready to create your pitching mind map. Mapping your pitch can help you be succinct in your delivery. Getting to the core of what your project is about is essential in a pitch. You want to hook the buyers with every sentence you speak. Your mind map will help you organize your thoughts and hone in on the key elements that are important. From your mind map, you can create pitching materials to make sure you convey what's most important.

When you are pitching, you want to emotionally pull at the buyer's heart. After all, creativity may start in the mind, but it lives in the heart until it's carried out. Therefore, one must persuade the buyer using the ethos of their project. This means your pitch will differ slightly contingent upon who you are pitching. Your goal should be to build into your pitch the very thing you learned in your research that emotionally connects your project to the person or company you are pitching. Ask questions like, *"What similarities does my project possess that connects me to the buyer, actors, or investor?"*

Additionally, before you can answer the question "*What should I say in my pitch,*" you need to know the answer to "*What do I want this buyer to*

walk away feeling and thinking about my project and characters?"
Mind mapping can help you develop the perfect pitch by marrying what matters most to your story to the person you are pitching. I have created a step-by-step process to help you mind map your pitch below.

1. In the center of the page write down the title of your show.
2. Underneath the title write what you want to achieve in your pitch. In other words, what do you want the receiver to walk away with? Ethos. Connect it with something emotional. An example of this could be *I want the buyer to understand what it is like to want to take your life. Or, I want the actor to connect to Mary's loss of a child.* Or you may write, *I want NBC to see how perfectly this show fits into their lineup. Or perhaps, I want them to understand what it is like to be a black man struggling with mental illness.*

More Examples:
- I want to show the afflictions of being transgendered.
- I want to paint a picture of what it is like to live with anxiety.
- I want to show the downside of being an entertainer.
- I want to show how moms really feel about motherhood without any holds barred.

3. Next, by drawing lines from the title outward, write all of the main or important characters.
4. Then, draw a line from the characters connecting what those characters want most in your story.
5. Draw another line from what they want most to what is getting in their way.
6. From the title, draw lines connecting it to a list of the most important storylines you have written.
7. Follow this by connecting the storylines to how they go about getting what they want.
8. Write what will happen if your character doesn't get what they want by connecting it to #7.
9. Next, write down the universal themes of your story based on all you've brainstormed.

Congratulations! You've completed your brainstorming session!
Now that you have completed your mind map, in a Word or PowerPoint document create category titles by character names beginning with your main character. Underneath it, write out all of the ideas you have

clumped together for that character and list it underneath the category title.

Pitching Challenge #5

Today, you are pitching a production company from your wish list. Choose one. They've scheduled you for fifteen minutes. Do a mind map for this pitch. Ask yourself, *"How can I make the buyer or talent connect to my pitch? How can I achieve my pitching goal?"* Write out a list of ways to achieve your pitching goals.

Examples:

> ➤ I will discuss the film's themes by beginning with the story of the years of struggle and self-doubt the lead character has struggled with before changing herself into a man.

> ➤ I can begin with discussing the leads nervous breakdown after she finds herself in court and everything has been taken away from her including her children.

> ➤ I will juxtapose the rise and fall of Whitney Houston and Michael Jackson.

WAIT. Before you start recording your pitch, go back to all of your other pitches and create a list of the things you want to keep. Incorporate that into this pitch. Get your recording device and put 15 minutes on the clock. From the pitching mind map you've completed, use your final list of achieving your goals to pitch your executive. Your goal is to connect the buyer emotionally.

GO!

How did your pitch go? Did you feel you achieved your goal of making the imaginary person feel the spirit of your project?

Go back and make notes of your pitching practice. If there is anything you want to change make the notes now.

CHAPTER FIVE

Getting A Pitch Meeting

*If you aren't making mistakes then you are not doing anything.
I'm positive that a doer makes mistakes.*
—John Wooten

How to Know What They are Looking For

There are many people who don't know who to pitch their projects to because they are uncertain about the mandate of networks. Parts of me feel like not even a network knows what they are looking for until they see or hear about it first. Yes, they have a mandate that aligns with their mission, but when they find something amazing that wasn't in-line with what they were seeking, they buy in to it.

There are different reasons that influence their decisions on which shows they pick up and which they let go. It is all the more reason you have to stay in tune with what is happening in the entertainment world because it can help influence not only the type of content you write about, but who you add to your wish lists to pitch and how you appeal to the executives.

The influencing factors can come from what's influencing the demographics of viewers who watch their films or television shows, trending topics, and even whatever is happening politically in the world at the time. In fact, in an article in *The Hollywood Reporter,* Lacey Rose wrote about the effects the Trump election has had on network shows they choose to put on air. After reaching out to Kenya Burris to search for right-wing voices for their writer's room, ABC's studio chief Patrick Moran said, "There was no way I wanted to do something that was going to further divide this country." At ABC, a change in their development slate will be to better appeal to middle America. NBC is rethinking their development to focus on more "feel-good" content since the 2016 election. As one content creator asked me about the ever-changing mandate, "How does one know what networks are seeking if they are ever changing? Do you only pitch if you have a project that aligns with the mandate of the network or studio, or do you create a project based on the changes?"

There are ways to tell what a studio is searching for and it can only strengthen your storytelling skills if you create for a studio's shifting mandate. Most people come up with their wish list based on what is airing on television or what slate of films studios have put out in the past. One great way to know what networks in particular are seeking is to pay close attention to the Upfronts that are done each year. Upfronts are usually held each spring and are events where advertisers make marketing deals based on the projects the network has ordered. A content creator can pay close attention to what shows the network has picked up to get a feel for what direction it is headed in by dissecting the type of shows, the genre, and the themes of the shows, which helps determine if theirs is a good fit.

Additionally, according to Kissmetrics.com companies like Netflix use data and trends to determine what movies to choose and content to create. It also announces what programs they are keeping and cutting on a monthly basis. That news, which can be found in trades like Cynopsis and Variety, to name a couple, can help you get a better understanding of the type of programming that works best for them and see what you have that aligns with their current programming.

Last, you want to always make sure your show aligns with the mission of the networks or studios.

Cold Calling

A person begins their pitch way before ever getting into the room. As independent creators without representation, the one thing we can rely on to get our projects seen and heard aren't our laurels (unless of course the buyer is a classmate), but our creativity. There is never a time we should bury the creative side. In fact, in order to penetrate the wall, we have to be far more creative in the emails we send, on phone calls we make, and in person when we are networking, than we have to be in the pitch room. What we do first is what will get us in the room. One must be very crafty in these situations in order to land themselves in the room. Let me be clear, crafty does not equal gimmicky, stalkerish, or creepy, it means being perceptive, ingenious, and clever.

I'll admit that my journey to pitch 100 times was an uphill battle. It was a daunting day-to-day process. I found myself doing a daily Miracle Morning[5] ritual of affirmations, mediation, visualizing, and other things just to build myself up to tackle the rejection that I was sure to encounter. At first, or at least in the first ten calls I made, I sounded shaky and unsure of myself. I was still working out my script of what I would say to reach the right person. But around call number ten, I began to get the groove of what worked and what didn't work to get through to the right person, or to be told "no" sooner so I could start making my next call.

---

[5] Elrod, Hal. (2012) *Miracle Morning: The Not So Obvious Secret Guaranteed to Transform Your Life (Before 8am)*

Getting through the gatekeeper is a pitch within itself that one must endure before getting a chance to actually pitch your projects. In those early calls, the gatekeepers could tell that I was a content creator looking to get through that proverbial wall. They could sense a lack of confidence in my voice and were ready with a rehearsed rebuttal that would send me back to square one.

I remember my first victory. I called The Will Packer Production Company to speak to a development executive. I'd done my research on IMDBpro and learned who was on their team. Of course, when I called I got the executive assistant. I was more than ten calls in, though, and had figured out my pitch. I knew how to be concise, quickly summarizing who I was and what I wanted. I boldly asked for the head of development like I was supposed to.

Me: Hi, This is Squeaky Moore from Moore Squeaky Productions, calling for "first name only."

Assistant: Oh (slight pause) okay, hold on. (comes back to phone) Squeaky, what production company are you with, again?

Me: Oh, tell her its Squeaky from Moore Squeaky Productions.

Assistant: Moore…Squeaky… Ok, hold the line for me.

Head of Development: Hello, this is (first name only).

Me: ☺

When I spoke to the head of development I knew I had one shot to make a connection. On that call I shared with her who I was and that I had a fairly new production company. Then I stated my purpose, which was, *I am a content creator with about seven projects that were developed and I want to build a relationship with them (their company) and share a few of my show ideas, if possible.* Of course, she gave me the legal spiel about unsolicited materials. I was fine with that. I had done all I could to make a connection. There was nothing left to do. I was about to hang up the phone when she stated that she would perhaps be interested in hearing more about any smaller budget projects or digital projects I had. She instructed me to email her the synopses.

Me: ☺

The takeaway

Practice your script about ten times or more before you call your first company. You want to sound confident, bold, and in charge. By practicing your script before you make calls, you can potentially make more connections rather than losing them due to uncertainty. Only a few will get the opportunity to make a connection and you want it to be you.

...Pitch #17

The best way to get a pitch meeting is to ask for a soft introduction. Most of you might read that and do either one of two things:

1. Nothing. You may be too afraid to ASK.

Or

2. Nothing. You may not believe that sometimes all it takes is an open mouth.

I've written about this topic in articles and I've also suggested this very thing in most of my pitching workshops, and when I follow up with people to see if they have used their networks to get pitches, the answer is most of the time a resounding "no."

To test this theory, I decided to take my advice and ask friends to do a soft introduction. So, I asked a friend of mine (one very familiar with my work) if she wouldn't mind doing a soft introduction to the head of development at a production company, with hopes that I could pitch them. I knew she and the lady were associates, and I felt based on the company's previous projects and what they currently had in development that at least three of the television shows I had created could suit their directive.

You've heard the saying *"a closed mouth won't get fed"* haven't you? Well, taking my advice worked for me. After the introduction was made, I followed up to ask for a chance to pitch. As a favor, the executive responded that same day. She expressed how busy she was and told me to fill out their release form with more information about the projects I was interested in pitching. She said if she were interested in any of them, she would follow up with me and let me know which ones she'd like to hear about. That day, I filled out the release and sent six projects to her. I was confident that three of them fit, but the others I was unsure about.

I decided to include them just in case they were heading in a different direction. My submission included the title, genre, logline, and a brief synopsis.

A month passed and I didn't hear from her. Since I had recently interviewed then senior director of development at BET on the topic of when and how to follow up (you can read his entire interview in Chapter 8), I decided to reach out to her based on the fact that she said she was very busy. I didn't jump to conclusions that she was uninterested; instead I figured she could have forgotten about my email. I emailed to ask her when a good time would be for a brief chat.

Another twelve days passed before she emailed me to see if I had time to meet the following Thursday. She was giving me 15 minutes of her time! Honestly, I stressed out. Why? Well, because she hadn't said which project she was specifically interested in and I forgot to ask and was too afraid to email her back, which meant I had to prepare to pitch them all. Also, the thought looming in my head was I was developing a new relationship and this meeting could determine whether or not my network would grow and the door would be open for future ideas – relationships are everything! I was able to get past my bout with fear and create a one-sheet for guidance on all of my projects. Then, I rehearsed.

On the call (our meeting was by phone since the production company is in LA, and I'm in New Jersey), she sounded rushed. She said she had a deadline to meet that day. Crap. I asked her if she wanted to hear about any of the projects in particular. She stated that her company was interested in scripted content so to start there, but that I could choose which project to discuss. It was followed by another mention of her deadline; I knew there wasn't much time left. Oh the joys of pitching by phone! It was now or never. At that moment, I heard Robert Townsend's voice from when I pitched him blurting, *"Just tell me the story!!!"* So, I began telling the story of the strongest, most interesting character I'd written about. Then the next one and the next, until the silent alarm rang, telling me her time was up. Our speed dating pitch session was over. She said she would get back to me.

The next morning I found an email from my new contact asking me for a second "date." She asked if I had a series bible and a pilot script for my project with the intriguing character whose story I told first. She also expressed interest in another project too, to which I jokingly thought,

"Jeez, you are asking for a lot of goodies on the second date!" But for the sake of my characters, I decided to take one for the team and relented: *"Oh, what the heck, just take all of me… and my content."* I'm sure my characters will appreciate the possibility of playing out their lives on television.

My takeaways

1. Practice prepares you to have grace under pressure.
2. Always think of Robert Townsend in tough pitching situations and just tell your story.
3. Most importantly, start your story with the character that is the most intriguing to you. Start talking first about the character that is like the love of your life or a miracle baby that came into your life and changed your world forever.
4. Last, be prepared and have all pitch materials ready in case they request them. Just make sure you have registered them all with Writers Guild of America (WGA). Do not hand them over in the room. Let them know that you will email the documents. This way, you can make whatever changes are needed based on any new discoveries made in your meeting.

Pitch Wish List

When you were creating your show or film, did you have people who popped in mind while you were creating your characters? A wish list is exactly what it sounds like. It's a list you create with all the people you have ever dreamt could make your project a reality, and you create lists for more than just talent, you create them for all who you will want to sell your project to.

Creating a wish list not only helps to set everyone on the same level; it helps to organize your future-pitching journey. By listing prototypes that can play the characters in your project, you give your characters more meaning to the people reviewing your bible. It emotionally stirs the people you are pitching, especially if the talent you have on your wish list has done an amazing job in a similar project. It gives an idea to others how you envision the roles played. Now, everyone else can see the character role as you see it.

However, most of us don't think past who we want to play the lead role or what celeb to attach to our reality franchise·, is collection of media that's different but your wish list shouldn't only include talent. You may have experienced as an underrepresented, independent content creator that you have to wear many hats. Most likely your hats will range from acting as a casting director to an executive producer and sales agent. This is why it is important to make wish lists for every hat you wear. Aside from casting, if you are acting as a sales agent you may create a wish list of distributors you want to pitch or perhaps which film festival you want your film to premiere in. If you were acting as a packaging agent, you would create a list of directors or writers you want to commission. Make a list of everyone you want to pitch. Include talent, directors, producers, writers, investors, partnerships, networks, production companies, distribution companies, film festivals, digital spaces, and more. When you are ready to begin pitching, I suggest you start with your top choice for each, research them, and cater your pitch to them.

· According to Wikipedia, a media franchise is a collection of related media in which several derivative works have been produced from an original creative work of a film

Q & A: 7 Tips on Finding a Manager or Agent

"I have been writing for quite some time and have a number of scripts in various genres. I have also put out two short films that have both garnered success online. But I'm still having trouble landing an agent or manager. Do you have any tips for what I should do next?"

Great question. Someone I interviewed for my book recently told me to keep creating work so that we always have something current to talk about and brand ourselves with. To that I add we should make sure we keep working on and shooting new projects so that agents and managers see that we are always creating. It's been great advice that we need to listen to.

I'm not sure of what you've done already to attract their attention, but here are a couple of things that I'd do:

1. Ask someone you know that has a manager/agent to do a soft intro or to pass your info on to them. (Write out exactly what you want them to say to the agent.) This is the best way. Big ask!

2. Submit your two films to as many festivals as you can. It will help you gain prestige and potentially gain the eyes of an agent if chosen as an official selection. You must promote the hell out of each "official selection." Send newsletters, try to get write ups in blogs and interviews for podcasts. Do the work and find out how the themes of your project relate to bloggers/podcaster's missions and pitch why they should interview you about your projects. After every article, official selection, or interview update potential agents and managers – even friends who have agents and managers.

3. Research agents and see if you can find their social media handles. Learn more about them, what they do, where they go. Try to be in the same place. Have your elevator speech ready.

4. Go to film festivals even if your film isn't in it and make it your business to socialize with everyone. Learn what they do. Agents and

managers support their talent. They would be at a festival.

5. Go to screenings and premieres and network with everyone. Find out what they do. When you meet an agent, spend time building the relationship.

6. If you've written scripts, take very powerful scenes from your script and email or mail it to the manager one scene at a time, once a month. It's much easier to sit and read a two or three-page compelling scene than it is an entire script. They may connect to the scene and want to know more about you. If you send them several great scenes over a course of time, they will grow to trust your creative genius.

7. Last, consider focusing all your attention on creating and writing a really great film or show. Next, focus on pitching it to production companies, investors and talent. Once the project is shot and released or aired, use its success to appeal to agents and managers, if they haven't come to you first.

7 Things to Include in Your Email Pre-Pitch

So the question is, *"How can you use the same creativity with which you created your project to get you in the room?"* One way is by emailing. Like me, many of you will have to do a lot of emailing to see if you can further share your idea. Even if you have asked someone to do a soft introduction, you still have to connect with that person to share your idea and do so fascinatingly in order to get to the next level. You have to be smart and clever in your approach. Not the type of clever where you are pulling out a bunch of unfunny tricks from your archetypal hat, but crafty in how you use your research, themes, and mood and tone in your email. If you have the email of a person you want to pitch, there is a way you can email them and grab their attention and possible get a pitch meeting.

On my journey to pitch 100 times this year, I have learned to perfect my pitch in person and through emailing. Both are important pitches. When you are in the room, you have to shine. The passion you exude when speaking about your projects should be undeniable, but it's getting into the room that is the hard part. Pitching is not *all* about what you do in person. It is first about *how* you get in the room. Without one, there is no other. You have to *get* into the room to pitch, so it's important that you perfect your email pitch.

I want to make clear that by "email pitch" I mean the pre-pitch – pitching to entice the subject enough to let you get in the room. I don't mean pitching your entire project by email. I mentioned in an earlier chapter that I had a prospective client who was sending his entire pitch to the buyer via email in hopes of getting his show picked up or possibly getting an investment deal. He had a valid reason, which was he lived in a city where there was no one potentially to pitch, at least that is how he felt. I can understand why one living in a small town, in a state that doesn't have many entertainment outlets nearby could feel this way. My prospective client said that it worked to some degree; distribution companies did respond to him, but in many cases, the company would have misread his communication. I read some of his communication and I am unsure how the companies were confused by it, as it was pretty clear to me, but it could also be that I had spoken with him several times about his projects before reading his materials so I could fill in the missing pieces. This is a great example of why sending your entire pitch through email is a bad idea. The ultimate goal should be to get in the room so that you can best explain your show's concept. If getting in the room isn't an option because it could become very costly to have to travel to larger cities to pitch your projects all the time, I suggest at least asking to share your pitch by phone or a video/Skype meeting. Your passion can never show as well on paper as it does in person. Therefore, the goal should always be to get in the room or even on the phone to further sell your idea.

When writing emails to potential buyers or talent, your goal should be to sell the overall idea of your project so well that the person who has to buy into it is intrigued enough to request a call or more info. I've had several people ask me questions about what should go into an email to people and companies they are seeking to pitch. Below are seven things I usually include in my email pre-pitches. My emails change based on the relationships I've developed or how I was introduced to the person I am writing to, but essentially these are the ingredients that make a winning email. You can include them creatively in whatever order you deem best and by what works for the kind of project you have created.

1. Choose a subject line that will make them want to read further.

I was told by an urban blogger that he receives hundreds of emails each day and the first emails he chooses to open are the ones with catchy subjects. If you have someone who referred you, then I would start with "so and so suggested I reach out to you – 3mm film with Michael B Jordan to star." Or, "So and so said you would love my film's star Michael B. Jordan, brief chat?" Or you can lure them using your talent's name, "Jussie Smollett project seeking 3mm - 4mm already secured" or "NAME OF SHOW with Taraji Henson attached seeking to live on HBO."

2. Praise them for their recent work in the industry.

I always praise whomever I'm reaching out to on their recent work. I make it a habit to know what the person or company has been doing recently. I'm not saying that it always works, but it's worked in my favor more times than not to let the person know I am well-informed of their work. When I write this part, I don't hold back. I go all in. Here is an example of one that I wrote to the President of BET's development and programming department one year:

> Dear _____, your background in television is simply amazing! You are a true trailblazer and you inspire me as an entertainment lawyer-turned executive producer-turned executive in charge at BET! You are the epitome of a "Woman of power…"

I know, it's a bit much, but it's worth it in the end. The truth is, I'm not lying. I really did feel this way about her work. When I write my praises of people, it is the things that connect me to them either from what I have seen at a glance or what I have read that I usually use when singing my praises, often from the research I've done of the person. I like to be genuine about the things that I write and suggest you do, too. Find your angle, that thing you connect with, and write about it in your email. My philosophy is to "go all out." Don't hold anything back in this section. Flattery wins.

3. Indicate you created this show specifically for their audience.

If it is an actor, company or network, I always let them know that I created this project specifically with them in mind. Nine times out of ten, it's true and even if you didn't create the content specifically for them, I'm certain that you think that particular person, network, or company must be right for your project otherwise you wouldn't have added their names to your wish list. Here is an example of what you would say.

Ex: "Hi, I've created a half-hour sitcom specifically for your female audience..."

4. Give the working title and a brief, generic synopsis of your show with a few themes.

When you are not represented and are making a connection to a network or production company, most do not want a synopsis until after you have signed a release form. But when you are enticing the buyer you can show how their audience will connect to your project by giving a generic, but enticing, synopsis. In other words, you would spell out a problem that the characters would find themselves in in your project. Your story will tell the themes of the project without necessarily saying, "The themes of my show are..."

An example I can use is *Sex and the City*. If I was sending an email to a perspective buyer, I might say:

> Imagine a show that depicts women living out their sexual exploits with no holds barred. No judgment, right? Well, the four women in *Sex and the City* experience love, pain, orgasms, and even a sexually transmitted disease or two in this one-hour dramedy..."

5. Show them through a one-liner that you've researched their audience and understand their demographics.

"This dramedy appeals to your 44% 23-30-year-old, female demo. It is a show that takes place in New York city, one of the fashion hubs of the world, and will charm your other female demos and fashionistas; after all, many of them live by the sentimentality '...there is nothing you can't do if you are in New York, New York, the city of dreams...'"

6. Let them know what else you have in your pipeline and what you have done (genres and themes).

In order to gain credibility in entertainment as a creator and in production, you want to tell the story of where you are in your career as a content creator. Letting them know that you have more says that this isn't your first rodeo and you can create repeatedly. Also, they may not be interested in what you are trying to pitch them, but something else in your pipeline may align with their mandate. You never know, sometimes it can be the thing you least expected, but it's where their company is headed. This has happened to me twice! The project I was least expecting the company to be interested in was the one they inquired about.

7. Give a specific date and time you want to chat with them.

"Are you available for a brief chat this week? A 15-minute call?"

I've had huge success with sending emails with the above contents in them. I don't always use every one of these in every email. You have to be wise in determining which email deserves what based on the relationships you have established already. For instance, in one email I sent, I had already been e-introduced to a person at a production company through a mentor friend of mine. After making the connection, I reached out to schedule a meeting with the person about possibly working with her on some of her productions or perhaps in development at her production company. Our meeting had been pushed about two times and she was doing a bunch of traveling as one of her shows was in season. She was very busy. One night I had an idea that one of my reality show concepts could be perfect and that night I reached out to her to request a pitch meeting. My email was very vague and yet enticing.

"SUBJECT: A show concept that fits your brand!

Hi xxxx,

How are you?

I was going to wait until our upcoming meeting to discuss this show concept that I put together, but it's really ready to go. The style and theme would fit perfectly with the xxxx brand and the type of projects I love producing.

Are you in New York and available to hear it briefly the week of March 16?

Oh by the way, I love the xxxx show. Xxxx (talent) is something else!

As you can see, I only used three of the seven suggestions above: the subject, praises, and specific date. You too will have to determine which are the best options for your emails that you send. Here is another example of an email:

Dear Xxxx,

Xxxx, who works in marketing at your company, suggested I reach out to you regarding some recent content I've created. I'd love to speak with you about the opportunity.

My name is Squeaky Moore. I am a showrunner, writer, and director, and have come up with a digital show concept specifically for your audience! I believe my web series, (name of project) would be great for your sub-channel (digital company name) and even the (company name) audience. I would love to further discuss this opportunity. Are you available this week for a brief chat? I have included a synopsis of the web-series below:

Working Title: xxxx

Logline: xxxx

Nadine Jones is turning 40 and life for her just turnt up; upside down, that is. She's about to give birth to her second child after it took six years to figure out how to properly mother her first born. Everything seems crazier the second time around, and at 40, Nadine has very little tolerance for, well...anything. xxxx

The (name of project) is a dramedy told in under three minutes, about (description of what the project is about). Each episode serves as a stand-alone as they (further explain).

Just make sure to do your research, be creative in email writing, and be ready to lay it all on the line in your praises.

CHAPTER SIX
The Pitch Meeting

The willingness to fail is a prerequisite for success.
—Mark Batterson

Pitching Challenge #6

Today you are at a speed dating pitch fest and have a short amount of time to sell your project to the buyer. The buyer sits in the seat across from you.

1. First, from your wish list, pick a potential buyer (network, studio house, production company, investor, or talent).
2. What is the first thing you will do when you sit down?
3. What are the first three things you will mention about your project? List them in the order you will say/pitch them.
4. Last, what do you know about the potential buyer? Any commonalities between them and your project? Incorporate anything you know about them, their company, or network into your pitch.
5. Put five minutes on a timer and practice the pitch you just wrote out.

Go…

Follow-up questions:

1. How do you feel about the results of your pitch?

2. Any discoveries?

3. What parts of your pitch do you want to keep?

4. What parts of your pitch need work?

Now go back and listen to pitch #1. How did you grow? Write out your successes and the things you'd like to keep from this pitch.

Pitching is an Art Form

The biggest problem most content creators have with pitching is they leave the creativity out of it. After spending months creating an amazing script with three-dimensional characters and an amazing world for them to live in, content creators decide to throw it all out the door and look for the stiffest suit they can find to go in to a pitch meeting. We go from being creative to acting as if we work on Wall Street, in the financial district, and are in a meeting talking about financial reports. It does not make any sense. Yet, I have made this mistake before. This is probably the biggest mistake content creators can make when pitching their projects to the buyers. Why become a suit now?

For instance, say you've spent several months (or years) writing about the hilarity of a mom who can't stand kids, including her own, and then you pitch that same show lacking humor. It would come across as if she is a woman who just buried her children. WRONG! Those are two different shows. The mom who cannot stand her own kids could be funny. The woman who comes across lacking humor could appear to want her kids six feet under, which would be some sort of drama or psychological thriller! It would be a very confusing pitch.

Everything about your pitch should come across the same exact way as it does in the script you have created. Comical, not dramatic. The same goes with your pitching materials. When pitching, try to replicate the mood of the project you have created in the materials and the pitch.

Also, pitch the characters based on the writer's attitude about who they are. Are they charming? Were they written to be jerks? Cunning? Submissive? Dark? When you are pitching them, however you pitch the characters, they should come across the way they were written. You can pitch your characters' attributes by giving examples of things they would do and say. I read a great example of "showing" character attributes in a pitch from an article written in *The New Yorker*. The article was written about STX Entertainment's studio head Adam Fogelson, about the producers of *Unmanned* who pitch them their film. In this case, they brought in their talent, Keanu Reeves, who does a great job expressing who he is through his actions. It reads:

> In the *Unmanned* meeting, Keanu Reeves suggested that they could build up a flashback scene where Royce visits his brother in the hospital after rescuing him in a firefight. "I'm on morphine, I'm fucked up, he should have let me die, maybe he gives me a little fucking Teddy bear, because our relationship has *that* thing" – he banged his fists together. He stood and began to pace, talking the story through. He became Bellam, tagging along behind Royce's ape in Hong Kong, limping, heroic, then became Royce's ape, looking back coldly: "C'mon, keep up!"

In this example, Keanu creates the mood by his actions. He also uses

81

language that tells more about who the character is. Why does this example matter to you? Well, it matters because you want the buyer to feel close to what you want the audience to feel in the movie theaters watching your movie, or someone sitting on their sofa watching your television show. You want to be able to engage the buyer as if they were watching this story for real. Also, how hot is it to have your talent acting out their roles! It shows that they are totally into the project.

Do Your Research

There is a lot of research that you can do to gain a better understanding of your project before pitching someone. You can use your research to help you create your wish lists for packaging and for pitching. Most of the time content creators create wish lists based on certain movies or televisions shows they have seen that resemble their own project; they choose the actors, directors, production companies, and executive producers that spawn from those films or televisions shows, and that's a great start.

However, there is much more research that one can do to broaden or expand a wish list. The research I am speaking of may help produce out-of-the-box ideas for content creators for pitching. Doing your research will ensure you are not pitching the wrong networks, production companies, executive producers, writers, and directors. The first bit of research a content creator can do is learning more about the person they are planning to pitch. One can usually tell what projects someone else is interested in by what he or she has already attached himself or herself too. But only looking at that can lead you astray. Suppose the person you are targeting has grown tired of doing projects with that same theme. Suppose the person, network, or company you are targeting wants to go down a different lane. Yes, by researching their IMDB pages you can learn a lot about the type of projects a person usually will take on, but if you research articles and q & a's that have been written on that person, company, or investor you can learn much more about the direction they want to go in or about their passions. This allows you to appeal to them through whatever similar connections they may have in relation to your project.

Social media pages can tell a lot about people, too. By researching a talent or an investor's social media, you can learn more about what charities they attend, if they are spiritual, if they are family-oriented, if they like motorcycles, whether or not they are sports fans, and much more. You can use what you learn to create a wish list and build your pitch for them specifically catering it toward their passions.

Let's say your film is about a woman fighting to save her child's life from a crippling disease. A little research can inform you that Jessica Alba may be a better choice than Jennifer Lawrence for the role based solely on the fact that Jessica is an advocate for children and families. If your project is about an activist fighting for civil rights, after a bit of research, you may find that Jessie Williams (*Grey's Anatomy*) may be a great person to approach to act as your film's lead.

While seeking funding for a documentary film I was producing about mental health, I researched talent who had a heart for mental health. I later approached mental health activist and author Terrie M. Williams and a man known as America's Psychologist, the media personality Dr. Jeffrey Gardere (CNN, *Housewives of Atlanta, Love and Hip Hop*). All of the things you learn from their social media pages can inform you on how to appeal to them in your pitch.

Additionally, you should do the same kind of research for networks. A common issue network executives have is that they receive pitch requests for shows that they would never do. In other words, if you are pitching a gospel network and your show is filled with cursing…well, that could reflect negatively on you. It could look like you are clueless or desperate. Your lack of research can hurt you in the long run. Remember, it only takes one mistake to lead them to an unfavorable first impression. Something as small as not doing your research on the company could make an executive decide not to hear you out anymore.

A marketing and brand strategist and mentor of mine, Sybil Clark Amuti, gave me such great and unique advice on researching investors. Sybil advised that once you lock in on an angel investor you are interested in, find out what their hobbies are:

> I like to follow their money because people put their money into their interests, into the things they are passionate about. Investors invest in the things they love first, the things they use. Look at the charities they like and connect with the people on the board. Investors are mission-minded. They spend their time and resources to invest in what matters to them.

It was really great insight she gave to me.

Last, research and know the lingo and buzz words. Is your show a half-

83

hour comedy or a format? Is it an episodic or is it a half-hour live action? Is it a docu-hybrid reality show or a knockout format competition? You should know what kind of show you are pitching. You should know the difference between a format show and a hybrid with a soft format. If you speak the language in an email, then the reader may think, *"Oh, this person isn't a novice."* Or maybe you hit the nail on the head for exactly what they are seeking so it sparks an interest. It sets you apart from many who don't know the lingo. You can Google the information. It's on the web — everything is on the web. But you have to put in a little time to research.

Practice Your Pitch

Put a timer on and practice pitching for 30 seconds, and then for three, five, and ten minutes to make sure you are ready for whatever time they give you. This will also show you how you do under the pressure of a timer. You'd be surprised at what you learn about your own project. One may ask, how long should my pitch be? If you practice pitching all of these times, then you are ready for an elevator pitch or a 30-minute pitch. You should be prepared for anything to happen. There is no cookie-cutter answer to how long a pitch should be. I've had as little as five minutes to pitch and as much as an hour! You want to be prepared for whatever time you have. There is no answer for how long your pitch should be; it can be as long as you keep the person interested and asking questions, which is the goal.

You can practice your pitch using your mind map, starting with the most important details first. You should practice hooking the buyer with your first line and build outward from there with your next important detail. Remember, rather than giving the facts, tell the story. Do not read line-for-line from a sheet of paper or a pitch deck!

If you practice your pitch several times, it will become more concise. You want to get the story in your heart. Think about it like this. You are your audience. What would grab you about your story? Start there and build outward telling the next best thing, and the next, and the next. This way you know you expressed all of the best information first and you don't waste time talking about random details instead of mentioning the most important parts.

Rehearse the Talent

It's important to rehearse with your talent because many of you will work endlessly on practicing your pitch and forget to work with the potential talent. If you rehearse your pitch but never take any time to prepare your talent on how you plan to pitch, it can be a disaster. If you are pitching unscripted projects, then your talent is a key factor in whether or not a buyer will buy into your show. A network is looking to see how charismatic your talent is and how willing they are to open their lives to the public. If your talent is none-the-wiser about elements or aspects of the show – or worse, they don't have an idea of how you plan to expose them – and they go into a pitch meeting and are not able to answer any questions or feel embarrassed by some of the executives questioning, then a network will assume they aren't fully on board.

Likewise, if you've packaged a film with a named actor and bring them into a pitch meeting and they are completely "in character" it could be the very thing that seals the deal with the producer to green-light your project. Seeing them live in the moment of the character you are pitching may bring your pitch to life. No matter what your project is, you should always rehearse your pitch with the talent so they are completely in the know.

Magilla TV Pitch: Don't Assume Anything

A year before writing this book, I sat in a room filled with hungry content creators looking to get more information on showrunning, or perhaps to meet some amazing women who could help take their content to the next level. I was in the room for both reasons. New York Women in Film and Television produced an event called "Women Who Run the Show." I boldly reached out to Tracy Baker Simmons to see if I could attend as a guest of hers. It was a bold move, as I was still developing a relationship with her. Had she said "no," I would have paid anyway. I just wanted to let her know that I was a fan of her work. She said, "Yes" and added me as one of her guests. Thinking back, that gesture was so nice of her. I sat in the room and listened to an amazing panel of women showrunners from shows like, *Who Wants to Be a Millionaire*, *The Suzy Orman Show*, and Magilla TV's, *Jersey Couture*.

As I sat and listened to the women speak, I made a list of the women I wanted to make a connection with. My goal wasn't to connect with them all, but to connect with a couple that could help see my pipeline of content through to the next level. I wasn't the best networker at this time and had lingered around until the last moment, almost missing my opportunity to meet with the owner of Magilla TV. She was clearly ready to leave, but she took a final breath and said hi. I told her I would

85

love to share some TV show ideas I thought were in line with what they usually put out at Magilla. I was quick to follow up with her. The next day, I reached out to her for a pitch meeting. I wrote,

> Subject: We met at, "Women Who Run the Show" NYWIFT event.
>
> Hi xx,
>
> How are you? We met at the "Women Who Run the Show" event that NYWIFT held. I loved all you had to say that evening! I'm writing because I would like to present an opportunity for a show concept I've developed that I believe could expand upon the type of projects you are already producing at Magilla and projects I love producing.
>
> Are you in New York and available to hear about my show idea(s) the week of April 13th?
>
> Oh, by the way, congrats on "I Got You Babies!" That show sounds very interesting and I can see moms around the world tuning in!
>
> Looking forward to seeing you next week.

I was excited when the owner followed up with a message that she'd introduce me to the development team to set up a meeting. I decided to prepare four pitches for my meeting with them.

I sat across from two of their development team members and pitched my number one show idea; the team liked it but it wasn't right for them. Then, one of their team members, a guy named Chris, said, "Your email stated you had 'ideas,' what else you got?" I started pitching the other show ideas. None of them were right. Finally, another woman in the room, said, "What about that piece you did on mental illness?" She had done her research. She was referring to a documentary short film I had co-created with a friend of mine. I paused for a minute to take that in. Then I went into pitching what I felt could be a great television docu-series with some of the same themes that were in the short film. It was a project that I always felt should be on television, yet I never developed a show around it. I went with the moment. I created an idea off the top of my head. They were interested. They offered a suggestion regarding the focus of the show and asked if I had the talent attached, and I told them I did. My talent, Dr. Jeff Gardere had given us his time while we were shooting the feature film, so I assumed it was a yes for television too. They wanted me to come back in with Dr. Jeff.

When I left, I immediately called Dr. Jeff to tell him the good news: a production company wanted us to come back in to pitch them. Well, Dr. Jeff couldn't commit. He was the face of another show that another well-known production company was pitching and had been given funding to shoot a pilot.

My lesson: Don't assume.

Just because Dr. Jeff was committed to our documentary film didn't mean he was committed to our television show. I should have communicated to him that I was pitching the idea and asked him if he could commit to it first before offering his name. It made me appear a liar. I went back to Magilla TV with my tail between my legs and told them Dr. Jeff had me on a hold to see if another show he'd committed to would be picked up. I guess they were used to this sort of thing happening because they told me they understood and to reach out should things change.

Be Open to Critique

I was meeting with Tracey Baker Simmons, the Executive Producer of *The Houston's* franchise, to discuss the format and bible I had created. And, even though it was hell to create, I looked on the bright side – *hey, I got to the next steps with her and have possibly begun packaging my TV show idea with an executive producer. Yay.* This EP also happens to have been the head of a development team for a production company.

We talked through my 20+ page format bible and she questioned a few of my creative decisions, ones that I may want to consider changing. She left the decision up to me, which meant if I changed them I had more work to do.

Her development thinking cap was on big time, and she forced me to think of the uniqueness of my show and how it fit into the years to come. She got me to think about how I can reinvent the ways this typical format has been done in the past. (GRRR... I thought I had done that.) Sigh. Being told that my idea isn't perfect is the part I used to abhor when I started pitching. I'm learning to get over myself. Okay, so...I'm not perfect! It isn't the end of the world. (Well, I eventually landed on this way of thinking. At first I was crushed to learn this news!) The biggest lesson I learned this time around was that no matter what, I'd have to spend time developing my idea to fit whoever I was pitching.

In minutes she brainstormed all of the unconventional, yet brilliant and relevant new innovations that shaped the future and how we could incorporate them, turning my show into a trendsetting and amazing idea.

Did you pick up on the _WE_ like I did? BINGO!!!!!

I still have a lot of work to do as I package this show and get it on air. But, _WE'RE moving_ in the right direction.

My takeaways

Don't feel dejected when asked to reconsider new ideas. It's not a form of rejection. It really means your concept has potential. It means you are in the beginning of a potential development deal! It isn't a *NO*, it's a *MAYBE SO* – provided you are willing to collaborate and open yourself up to possibilities. Trust me when I say it took me two years to realize this lesson, which is a mistake I don't want you to waste time on. So, if you are in development, accept it as a great possibility and do not allow your hurt pride or stubbornness to get in the way of your potential greatness.

A Step-By-Step Example of How to Pitch

To help you further, let me walk you through a potential pitch meeting from beginning to end. I thought it would work best if I gave you specific examples. From start to finish, you can at least have an idea of what to expect when going into a meeting.

In many meetings the first couple of minutes are going to be small talk, unless for some reason you are at a speed dating pitch, or the buyer has a hard stop and you have a specific amount of time to pitch and are racing against the clock, at which point you want to get right down to business.

The first thing you want to do is introduce yourself. Next,
As you move into your pitch, come up with a great hook that you can use to draw them in. It can be an engaging question that will make them think and respond to you, but you want to go in strong and grab their attention.

Then you want to go into storytelling mode. You can start with the premise, or you can start with talking about your most compelling character and what starts them on the journey, or you can decide to pitch an episode from start to finish.

After you tell what the story is about or a potential storyline, you can choose to build the format of your project into the story or explain the format and/or structure of your project afterwards, explaining what viewers can expect to see moment to moment, especially if it is a reality, format, or television show. If it is a film, break your story down based on acts and let your storytelling build as it would if they were watching it.

If you bring talent to the pitch meeting with you, allow for them to join in on the conversation by interjecting their input at certain moments, going further into the storytelling piece, and showing their dynamic personalities or acting skills. You want to allow the buyers to see that the talent is fully invested.

At some point in your storytelling, check in to see if the buyers have any questions so that you can erase any confusion that may have arisen. If questions or statements happen to come up during the pitch, you want to be able to address them and allow the pitch to turn into a dialogue. It's important to know your story inside out so that you can get off track if you need to when questions are thrown your way.

After your storytelling is done, go through potential episodes and/or act structure, leading them on the journey to the climax of your project. Check in again and invite them to ask more questions.

After all of the questions have been asked and answered you want to be able to close and these are six steps you can do to make sure you close well.

Six Ways to Close Your Pitch Meeting

1. Before you leave the room make sure you've asked if they have any questions. Asking this question allows you to clear up anything that was unclear or confusing. The goal is to make sure the buyer has all they need to know to carry your project to the next person up.

2. Ask if they want to hear about any other related information you've come up with regarding your project. For example, you may say, "Would you like to hear about some of the ideas I've come up with to market this project?" Or you may say, "Would you like me to tell you some of the cross promotional ideas I've come up with?" This lets the buyer know you've thought through every aspect of your project.

3. Give a recap of anything they ask you to do so that you have clear instructions on what to do next. If you were unclear about anything, it can be cleared up before you leave.

4. Ask them, "What are the next steps?"

5. Shake hands.
6. Follow up with a great email. Include action items requested, thank them for their time and let them know how amazing their team was. Add a note about yourself further explaining a skill they don't already know you have or a special fun fact. Then ask again, "When should I expect to hear back from you?"

What to Leave Behind

If you are having a great pitch meeting, it may mean that suggestions are flowing from everyone in the room. It's a good sign and could mean the buyer really likes your idea and therefore is brainstorming the possibilities. Afterwards they may ask the question "Do you have a one-sheet or a bible you could give me to share with the rest of the team?" If you find yourself in this situation and want to know what to do, my suggestion is to leave nothing behind after your meeting except for maybe a business card.

The reason you shouldn't hand over any materials while in the room is simple. Let's say your potential buyers have expressed interest in your project, but have mentioned certain themes they thought it should tackle, or perhaps suggested that you add more drama in the episodes, or a more specific suggestion, you want to take the materials home so that you can make all necessary changes. If you hand over your materials as is, the changes that were discussed may never reach the other team members or might get lost in translation, causing your project to get passed on. You want to be able to make all necessary changes to your materials based on the conversation you had during your pitch meeting. In this case you would say, "Yes, I have them, but I would like to make a few changes before I do." It allows you an opportunity to ask questions that you may have forgotten to ask during the initial meeting. At this point the ball is in your court and you can continue to build upon your relationship.

After you have made adjustments to your documents, you should draft an email to thank them for the opportunity to share your project, praise them for being an amazing bunch of people, and ask all of your questions (especially, "How long will it take from this point," or "What should I expect next?" Or any questions you may have forgotten to ask during the meeting. By doing this, you keep control of the conversation. Keeping your materials allows you another chance to connect with the buyer and for you to keep yourself and your project at the forefront of their minds.

I received this awesome advice from WE TV's EVP of Development & Programming Executive, Lauren Gellert, at an invite-only producer event and thought it was just genius: "give more information about yourself that you weren't able to give in your meeting." Let them know in the email any useful, relevant, skills you may have. Giving your email this extra touch after your pitch meeting is sure to separate you from others who are following up on their pitches. If nothing else, it can open you up for other opportunities to work with the network and allow you to continue to build the relationship with them; hopefully this will allow you to know the right time for the perfect project that fits their network.

Four Pitches in One Week

Pitch #74

It would be over a year before I reached out to Magilla TV again. It was during a pitch with a development executive at Rainforest Entertainment that I decided to focus on the mental health piece that Magilla TV had first expressed interest in. The executive at Rainforest was interested in the project too and they weren't the only ones interested; Tracey Baker Simmons reached out to me one day and asked if I was doing anything with the mental health piece because a network had expressed interest in the topic. It was then I decided to put some serious time into developing a show around mental health.

After I spent time developing it I reached out to Dr. Jeff, who was still waiting to see what would happen with the other show. He asked me if I could wait a few months before he could commit. I was done with waiting. I began looking for another well-known host, though I felt no

91

one would be more charismatic than Dr. Jeff. I let Dr. Jeff know that I would be moving on and couldn't wait anymore. A couple of months later Dr. Jeff and I saw each other at Urbanworld Film Festival. He expressed his interest in the project again, he let me know he was on board; his show was on hold because the network was undergoing major changes. I immediately reached out to Magilla TV. I reminded the executive of what had come out of our meeting and asked him if they were interested in me pitching them a newly developed show that incorporated their suggestion to build it around teens, and that I would bring my talent, which at this time was Dr. Jeff and cohost, Dee Marshall, a life coach. It took about two weeks to schedule a meeting.

I drew inspiration from Keanu Reeves for our docu-reality show pitch. I knew it would be a unique one, especially done out of the context of a film. Since I knew they wanted to personally meet the talent, I had the talent act out what a potential scene in episode five and seven in the format would resemble. After much deliberation, my partner and I decided these two episodes would make the best stories to tell in the pitch meeting, based on our research. It was a very fun pitch meeting. We engaged the development team completely.

Pitch #75

Days later, we pitched WE TV at an invite-only producer meet and greet event. Our team (the mental health one) had rehearsed to fine-tune the pitch, this time choosing to pitch the pilot episode and play out what it would resemble. The executive stopped us mid-pitch and told us that it was the best pitch she'd seen that day, after stating, "And we see a lot of pitches!"

Pitch #76

On this same day, I had a call with an executive from Centric TV. There were three different line items on my agenda I wanted to cover, one of which was to do an elevator pitch of the mental health show idea, starting with season two's theme that centered on women since it was a woman-centered network. The executive expressed that their audience always asked for shows like the one I was pitching, but they didn't show up to watch them, and they never received good ratings from these types of shows. I appreciated that information. I didn't feel let down at all. While it would be great to be green lit, it would have crushed me to see my show piloted but followed by a meeting to say they weren't going to order more episodes. I knew I wanted my show to live on for subsequent seasons. I wanted syndication. I was completely fine with what she had to say. That show wasn't right for them.

What happened next was a God moment. As we were talking about this book and my bigger stretch goal of helping women and minorities get more of their projects on air, an idea formed in my head for a new show. She seemed just as excited about the idea as I was. She informed me that Centric was going through a facelift and we agreed to check back in two months, which would give me time to develop the idea we'd brainstormed. That meeting confirmed that I had grown. I was no longer the woman who shut down from feelings of rejection; it confirmed that hearing the word "no…" may just mean "not yet…or not quite right."

Pitch #77

I also reached out to Mona Scott of Monami Entertainment (who I always found pleasant and receptive) to see if she would be interested in hearing more about the show I'd developed around mental health. I knew from a discussion with her that she was looking to expand her brand and a member from her team confirmed it when I pitched her the show idea. She too liked the idea, my passion behind the idea, and how well I'd pitched the show. She asked me to send over the show bible so she would be able to pitch it to her team.

It had been a busy but delightful week. By this time, between pitching talent, network executives, investors, production companies, networks, and other companies for sponsorship and product placement deals, I had pitched close to eighty times. I thought about my earlier pitches and how much time I would lose between pitches before stepping out to pitch again. It was close to 80 pitches in when I observed how much I had changed. I'd had a total mind shift around my creativity, how I valued myself and my work, and my faith in God. The biggest conclusion I drew from it all was that the only way to become successful was to continue putting myself out there. The probabilities were much higher this way.

There are a lot of takeaways in the pitching stories above. I'd tell you, but I think it would be more beneficial for you to write down a few of your own takeaways.

CHAPTER SEVEN

Optioned, Go to Series or Pass: What You Can Expect

All the best things that happened to me happened after I was rejected. I knew the power of getting past no.
—Barbara Corcoran

Follow your bliss and the universe will open doors where there were only walls.
—Joseph Campbell

Getting a "We Pass"

Some of you reading may have wondered what happened with the BET pitch. Well, on the same day we sent Austyn the email asking for them to sign an NDA, he politely passed on the opportunity stating that he had "soft-balled the world" to his team. He mentioned already having shows in development and our show being a little *repetitive*. He thanked us again for painting such a "clear world."

What a blow to the gut!

Nine times out of ten, you will hear these words if you are a content creator and are selling your ideas for the big and small screen. That first pitch with BET was an emotional roller coaster of wins and losses! I remember it as if it was yesterday! By God's grace, my writing partner and I were able to get through the proverbial "Wall of Jericho"· without having representation and into the doors to pitch our big idea! Already this was a BIG HUGE WIN!

As I wrote before, with our pitch to BET we worked tirelessly to create the world of our show and to create interesting and unique characters and how their worlds collide. The win here was that it resonated with the development person. His words were, to be exact (Yes, I remember them verbatim. It was my first real validation that I had talent!) He said, "You have created a great world for your characters. People usually only focus on great characters!" The network executive offered us our next steps, which were to pitch the higher-ups.

In fairness and honesty, the executive Austyn Biggers had said in our meeting that the network had a couple of projects in development with similar themes, so we were aware of what we were up against, but the executive felt our show was pretty good and wanted it to go to the next level. He was so gracious; he even offered us an opportunity to prep with him before pitching his team.

We were excited! I felt I could see the light at the end of the tunnel. All of our preparation and pitch rehearsals had paid off. Did I mention how excited I was? If I can be brutally embarrassingly honest, I'd even visualized myself riding in a stylishly swift new car driving all the way through the gates of my new mansion! (Don't laugh at me, I'm a

---

· According to biblical history, in Joshua 6:1-27, the walls of Jericho fell after Joshua's Israelite army marched around the city blowing their trumpets.

dreamer, and that's okay because it helps me as a writer.) I knew in the pit of my soul this was it, my breakthrough moment.

Imagine how I felt when we received the email that the higher ups had decided to "pass" on our show. No need to imagine. I can share with you how I felt. I felt like a black hole had come and sucked away all of the life, ambition, dreams, positivity, optimism, and any other words associated with winning out of me. Instantly, I completely felt like I had failed. At least, this is how that "we're going to pass" registered to me. Other feelings that followed were: "You're not good enough. You'll never make it. Your concept wasn't good, and Squeaky don't quit your day job," just to name a few.

The truth is I was too hard on myself. Just like most people do, I completely forgot about all of the positives and only focused on the pass. I hadn't thought of a plan b, should I hear the word pass. Hell, at the time, I didn't even know that was an industry term!

Here's what I wish someone would have told me to help get through the creative paralysis I suffered after this pass. It's the same plan I think you should follow if you ever hear "we pass."

Prepare a contingency plan before your pitch meeting that answers: What will you do if you are told, "We'll pass?" Your plan should include:

1. **A follow-up question.** You want to ask for the reasons why they decided to pass. You have to be open to the truth if you want to get better. Understanding the "why" could help a lot and save you time in preparing for future pitches. It could also take away your feelings of failure and any paralysis you may experience. I recently spoke with a person in development about this, and he confirmed that there is nothing wrong with asking this type of question. It shows your drive.

2. **A list of gratitude's.** Create a list of gratitude's before walking through that door to pitch. Write all the things you were grateful for before hearing that dreaded phrase. You should never forget your wins!

3. **A list of affirmations**. Create a list of powerful affirmations that includes "I have all the answers within me. This 'NO' is not

universal," and pick as many others that will inspire and motivate you and turn your thinking around. You want to remind yourself of the power within right away. Never leave your power with the people you've just pitched!

4. **Journal.** Mark Batterson writes in his book, *Draw the Circle,* "We have a tendency to remember what we should forget and forget what we should remember." Taking the time out to journal immediately after the pitch will allow you to remember all of the great things that happened and the things that need improvement. Be sure to remember all of the details: Who was in the room? How did the conversation flow? What you felt worked. Where you felt you need improvement. What did the person you pitched say? What questions were asked? What questions couldn't you answer? How did the meeting end?

5. **Plan of Action.** Create a plan of action that you will carry out should you hear that dreaded phase. Your plan of action should include:
   * Sitting for an hour or two of complete silence. You need time to think of your next steps so you can be most productive.
   * Giving yourself a time frame to fix all the things you felt went wrong in that meeting and any suggestions made by the network, if you agree with them.
   * Brainstorming a list of people or books that can help as a mentor to you while you are fixing your issues.
   * Doing all you can to set up your next pitch immediately, only allow yourself the necessary time to fix your problems! You want to do this so that you don't allow yourself to dwell in the rejection. Trust me, feeling paralyzed by rejection is real! It's said, the way to face fear is by doing the thing you are most afraid to do. Well, I feel the same about pitching. Face paralysis head on and move past it!

Should You Ask for a Non-Disclosure Agreement?

Quite frequently, content creators ask me if they should bring a non-disclosure agreement to their pitch meetings for buyers to sign. It's a tough question to answer. I have the heart of a content creator and have become sensitive to the dilemmas of honest development executives too. To give another example, a young lady I advise was meeting with a development executive at a production company and she was faced with this burning question as well. I shared with her what I learned by asking

97

for an NDA, and after our conversation she decided to ask the assistant of the person she was pitching to get a feel for how that executive takes being asked to sign NDAs from content creators. The assistant forewarned her not to ask the executive to sign an NDA for the same reasons I had.

This topic always makes content creators wary. Simply put, we are afraid to have our ideas stolen by the big entertainment conglomerates. What scares us are the countless stories of content creators whose ideas were stolen and held up in court for years seeking retribution for pay. There are many suits made about stolen stories and the films and TV shows in question are so close its scary and hard to believe that they were not stolen. We all feel we have the first and only story ever written about the subject we are writing about.

I remember when I first watched the sneak preview of *Empire* with the fabulous Taraji P. Henson. My body became hot inside because the story that I had been working on for two years and had poured so much of my time and attention into was playing out in front of my eyes. I called my writing partner back (she had already blown up my phone because she too felt the same way), and together we discussed our thoughts about how similar our show was to the one we were watching. We were very disappointed. Our show had made it on air. "They" had stolen it. The only thing was, we hadn't pitched it to FOX network. We had pitched it, but the development executives we pitched it to were still at the network we pitched it to. No one had stolen our idea. It was just a similar story, scarily, with a lot of the same elements. It was our rude awakenings to just how many "original" ideas were similar. It was my awakening that I couldn't afford to sleep on my ideas as I had done in previous years because just like I was creating amazing ideas, someone else was and pitching them too. Crap.

Funny enough, my writing partner went on to work at a production company and a content creator sent in a pitch stating that Lee Daniels had stolen their idea from a sizzle reel of their show that was shot before the pilot episode of *Empire* came out. The sizzle wasn't nearly the same show, but there were a few themes that were similar. Afterwards, several others came out of the woodworks about how *Empire* was stolen from them. My partner and I had a good laugh. Surely *Empire* hadn't been stolen from all of them. We redrafted our drama to go in a completely different direction.

In the examples above, I hate to say that the network executives and studio houses must have a tough time when it comes to a desire to hear new voices and stories and the potential threat for being sued. At the same time, I support content creators in some of the legitimate cases like in the case of *The Matrix*, *Avatar*, *The Purge*, *Good Deeds*, and other movies.

So, what do we do? Again, this is a very tough question and I can only offer what I do now that I have experienced being passed on after asking a network to sign an NDA, and watching Taraji play Pam (the character's name in the show I co-wrote. Lol) on air. I pitch without asking for an NDA.

It's a tough call to make. So I can't advise you on how to make it. But what I can advise is that you must be sure you register your projects with the Writers Guild of America (WGA). When I register my projects, I register them in their most completed draft. I register everything I have created for the project too, that is, the bible, the script, and storyboards if you have them, and look books. Register all of it. This way you have some protection. WGA has an East and West coast division you can register with for a very reasonable price (the cost of a very inexpensive dinner).

Austyn Biggers explained it to me best when he told me that the reason networks only take agent-arranged pitch meetings is there is a sense of trust that comes with an agency/network relationship that has been pre-established that isn't with the underrepresented content creator. The fear of intellectual property being stolen and asking the executive to sign an NDA is basically saying indirectly, *I'm not sure I can trust you*, in which case they feel, *why pitch someone you don't trust?*

Magilla TV Pitch

It had been almost two years since my first pitch with Magilla TV. My relationship with them began on April 10th, 2015. During my initial pitch meeting with them, one of the executives made a suggestion that the show I was pitching would be cool to see in the teen space. I took the note. I remained in contact with them and informed them when there was something worth mentioning. But it was at the beginning of 2017 that I reached back out to them. I had spent about a year toying with the suggestion and developed the mental health show with the focus on teens, as they'd suggested. Additionally, I created subsequent seasons with themes that didn't focus on teens, just to make the show more

99

viable. I wanted the option to flex it depending on who we pitched, and developed it so it could have franchise appeal. As I said in the previous chapter, the pitch went over well. They seemed to really love our pitch and were completely engaged during the meeting. I received a beautiful email (because their team really is awesome) that broke my heart…a little.

It read:

"Hi Squeaky,

Hope you are well! Apologize for not getting back to you sooner - took some time to get everyone back in the office, but we were able to bring the project up the chain.

Although the execs thought the talent sounded great (they really do have great energy and chemistry) unfortunately it's a pass for now. The age group the format focused on makes it difficult to go to multiple places with - and although there is the MADE element of the show it's still difficult to make the space more visual. That said I think you have something unique and wish you all of the luck pitching - I think you're trying to tell some very important stories.

Again, [we are] truly sorry for not getting back sooner. Our door is always open, you always bring exciting things our way!"

You know you've grown when hearing the words "it's a pass for now" doesn't register as a big sign of rejection, failure, I'm not good enough, or creative enough. After this email, I simply kept it moving. Knowing all that I know now about the game of selling projects has taught me to move on and to do it quickly. Now, I am able to see the wins in every situation. They were:

1. I've established a relationship with a production that appreciates my creativity.
2. They respect me as a content creator and have given me an open door.
3. They gave me sound advice to use if I wanted to move forward in a different way.
4. They gave me praise and said my ideas are exciting. This is always good for the ego.

100

5. They loved my talent and perhaps the talent may be enough for another buyer I pitch.

It's important to be able to quickly reframe your thinking after hearing that the buyer isn't buying. In the message above I counted all my wins and brought them into my next pitch meeting.

I replied quickly to her email letting her know that I was working on another show concept that I thought would fit well with their mandate and would reach out once I had developed it. Whether I really have an idea that is perfect for them or not is neither here nor there, what is really important is the open door policy that I have established.

Why Do Good Shows Get Passed On?

"Don't take it personal," says Austyn Biggers.

I needed answers even a few years after my BET pitch. So, when I spoke to former Senior Director of development at BET Networks, I asked him about this very subject. I asked a lot of questions, because having heard the words, "We'll pass," more than I'd like to admit, I wanted to know the reason behind why he and his team at BET pass on ideas, or at least the *real* reason they passed on me. His response was eye opening for me and I wanted to highlight it because I think it helped me to not take the pass so personally, and certainly not to give up on my ideas and myself because I'm told "not this time" by a network. I think it could help you too.

Squeaky: One big question I have is, what are some of the things that will cause great ideas to get passed over?

Austyn: I think one thing that would be kind of shocking to people is we pass on about 85% of everything we hear.

Squeaky: Even if it's good?

Austyn: A lot of times. Timing might not be right. You might be pitching a game show when I just bought three that I can't get out of. I'm already committed. Or you might be pitching me the best-animated show in the history of television, but we're not doing animation. I think the big thing with content creators and selling is don't take it personal. When I got to the network, [He was also a content creator], I realized why my shows didn't get to series – [because I did a couple of pilots but

101

they never went to series.] But, I realized it had nothing to do with me. It had nothing to do with my show or me. If you have the best show in the television, people will make room for it, and they won't make excuses. But a lot of times it's just, "Oh, they were interested in it, but at the time I made it, TV viewership changed. It's ever evolving.

We spoke a lot more about it, and it all boils down to this: Executives or whoever you are pitching may decide to pass on your idea, and it doesn't mean that it wasn't a great idea; it just wasn't right at that moment, for that particular buyer, so don't take it personally. But, definitely ask why they decided to pass. This way you can make a decision on how to proceed.

Getting Optioned and Going to Series

If your project was optioned or goes straight to series, congrats! They are both huge successes and worth a celebration. If you are called and told the producer wants to option your project you are well on your way. Getting optioned means that they are going to pay you to shop your project around in hopes of seeing if it can get made. Getting optioned does not guarantee that your film or show will get made, though. Your option agreement will determine how long the company has to get your project made before they have to turn the rights back over to you. At the end of the option agreement, the company will determine if they want to extend the agreement, if so they will have to pay you again in order to extend the time.

If you have been told, "We want to order 10 shows" or "We want this to go straight to series" do a dance right now! This means a network believes in your project so much they will potentially buy a season of your content to see how it does on air. This is a great position to be in because you have time to allow your project to garner a buzz. Just before the series order is up, and based on the ratings, the network will determine if they want to order another round of episodes. Let's pray that after reading and applying the principles in this book, you'll create a pitch so good the network will order a season of shows of your project!

CHAPTER EIGHT

From the Experts:
The Dos and Don'ts of Pitching

You know, God will give favor to anyone who will believe Him. Every day you should confess that you have favor everywhere you go. God will begin to open doors that you wouldn't believe.
—Joyce Meyers

A year and a half ago I began a rewarding journey to find the answers that could help content creators like you better prepare to pitch your projects so you could take control of your creative careers rather than sit on your dreams. In a culture that seems to shun 90% or more creatives from getting through the doors, my promise was to help as many as I could to at least understand what it takes to pitch and be heard by interviewing knowledgeable and creative executives and content creators. I've shared with you, as many defining moments of my pitching journey that I could think of, and other moments seem to come when I am in the act of coaching others. However, I thought it would be great to get insight from people in the business and ones who've actually bridged the gap with successfully pitching.

In preparation for the interviews, I polled some of your burning pitching questions and asked the executives and producers for answers in hopes to be enlightened about the process of pitching. In the following interviews, we discuss the dos and don'ts, nuts and bolts, and strategies for having an effective pitch. My hope is that these interviews can cover any loopholes that I may have missed and give different perspectives that my experiences have afforded me.

Austyn Biggers

Executive Producer, Development at Logo TV (Former Sr. Director of Development, BET)

Austyn Biggers currently serves as **Executive Producer, Development at Logo TV.** Former Sr. Director of Development for BET Networks, where he was involved in all facets of original series development and production. Austyn led a development team that concentrated on internal development and in-house production as well as third-party productions. Austyn's BET credits include *Baldwin Hills, College Hill, Keyshia Cole: The Way It Is, First In, Being Terry Kennedy, Born to Dance: Laurieann Gibson, Tiny & Toya, Let's Stay Together, The Sheards, P.S. The Post Show,* and most recently *Criminals at Work* for the network. Originally from Nashville, TN, Austyn attended Florida State University and has called Atlanta, New York, and London home before settling down in LA. Austyn volunteers with several organizations including those related to HIV/AIDS, women and men's cancer, and domestic abuse. He is also a strong advocate for animal rights and encourages everyone he knows to adopt his or her next pet.

SM: The last time we spoke [after our first pitch meeting], you said, "Let's prepare for the next meeting. I want you to meet with me first because I want to talk to you about a few things before you pitch the higher execs." You wanted to talk to us about storytelling. Can you tell me how storytelling relates to pitching?

AB: I think what you're looking for is my theory that first of all, content is king. But I said this to my friends in the business all the time, storytellers tell stories all the time.

Everything you're doing is telling a story. You might be coming and pitching me a show about a bunch of hotheads in Memphis. I might pass on that. But during that process, you really told me a story about who you are as a person. You told me a story about what type of shows you're interested in telling. You showed me a sizzle reel, which tells me a story of how you execute your idea and your vision. If you're truly a storyteller, remember that you're telling stories all the time not just when you're telling your story.

SM:	I get that.
AB:	The way you're dressed tells a story. The way you network tells a story. And as a storyteller, you've got to be conscious of what kind of story you're telling. It's almost saying, "If you're a content creator, you create content all the time including the best content in the world – your life." You create your life. You direct your life. You produce your life. You choose the starring people, who star roles in your life.
	I think the same way about a pitch meeting. The minute you come in, you're telling me a story. If I can say something to you that's slightly inappropriate or slightly jarring or mentioned my boyfriend and you have a rebuttal that's funny and witty, you're telling a story about what it's going to be like to work with you. As opposed to not being able to do that, then you're telling a story of, "This is not only somebody who only cares about their project as they're here to talk about, but they don't really have a story to tell about themselves." It happens a lot. Storytellers hide behind other people.
SM:	Right.
AB:	We hide behind our passion project. I don't know how many times people send me an email who are new in the business and the email is – let's say you have a show called One Hit Wonder and people would send me an email that's austyn@onehitwonder.com – that one project defines you as a content creator and you're not going to create anything else? And they live and die with their passion project. Sometimes there's a good reason. It might be about helping young African-American girls learn how to code and get into the tech industry. That's an admirable goal but should it define everything about you?
SM:	I get it. Just thinking about that makes me realize I must be more intentional about how I'm telling my entire story.
AB:	And that's the word right there, that's the word – intentional. You might luck out on a good meeting – you know the saying even a broke clock strikes right twice a day?
SM:	Yeah.

AB:	You might luck out on a good meeting if you're just a good bullshitter, but you can't do it consistently if you're not intentional about what you're doing. You can't just kind of shoot the shit.
	If your strategy is to come in and shoot the shit, then that's great. Do that but be intentional about it. Come in and say, "I'm not going to pitch you anything today. We're going to pitch you something but after I heard you guys talk a little bit, I realized that's probably not right for you. Now, I just want to get to know more about what makes you excited."
	I always love it in a meeting when somebody comes in – basically what happens to me all day is people come in and they pitch me a show that they are pitching three other networks.
	And they practiced the spiel and they got it going. What I always try to do early on is throw a wrench in the pitch, just get them off script.
SM:	Really?
AB:	If they're not passionate about repeating – they've all been going in the same order all the day. The agents spoke first and then the creator and then the producer and then the director.
	I just throw a wrench in all of it and I go straight and start talking to them. I love watching the producer's eyes just like start to freak out like, "Oh my God. We're off the script."
	But the truth of the matter is, we're making a show about your talent. And if you don't know how to coach your talent and take and answer about basic questions about their own lives, they know their story. I'm not asking them questions about a story that somebody else made up. I'm asking a question about them because they authentically know their story.
	What the directors and the producers are saying is their story may not be accurate and they may not know that well. And to be honest, half of the time I can tell, they haven't really spent much time with these people.
	Maybe they've got a junior development person working with them and now they're just ready to pitch and they just got up to speed two days ago. They've never even met these people. I can see that in the room.

107

SM: What advice would you give to better prepare for that?

AB: You have to know whatever you're pitching; you have to know the story. In order to know the story, you have to repeat the story a thousand times.

I say this a lot whenever I go to people and I talk to them in college and I say, "Think about it." Nobody likes to admit this, but everybody's got a lie. Everybody's got a lie that they have to tell everybody all the time. You tell the lie so many times that you don't remember if it was a dream or if it actually happened.

People in your own family will say, "That didn't happen." Everybody's got it. I don't think it's intentional.

SM: It's their truth.

AB: It's their truth. For me it was I and my brother burned down the backyard once when we were trying to barbecue. Now, in my small mind I pictured acres of woods burning to the ground. My mom was like, there's a little grass fire no bigger than 10 yards.

But I told that story so many times in my life and I'm a hero and that I actually saved my brother from being burned alive. If he told anybody, special services are going to come and take us from our mother. Everybody was like, "That never happened."

But because I told that story so many times, I feel that story. I dreamed that story. It's been in my mind. You can ask me anything about that day – what color was the blanket you put it out with? It was blue. I know it. I know it in my head.

I tell people all the time, you got to find that in you because the best storytellers are the best liars.

SM: I'm a huge daydreamer. If you are a daydreamer you know that where you start is definitely not where you end up. You can still be daydreaming the same dream years later.

Every time you close your eyes or every time you're thinking it through on a bus or a train or wherever you are and you've got time, you go back and paint a better picture.

AB: Right. More vivid.

SM: More vivid, it's so vivid and it becomes a better daydream. Honestly, that's a principle that should always be applied. Daydream your idea until it's fully developed.

AB: You sometimes pitch your show to people – I always say obviously, pitch to mama because mama loves everybody. And then, pitch it to that girl that you know doesn't like you because she's going to be honest about it. Ask that person to throw wrenches in it.

Let's say you're doing a script and you're telling this story about this secret agent who goes to Burger King and she orders a Whopper with cheese and that's some kind of a secret code word and everything started to happen.

I'm going to tell you right now, did she get fries? If you don't know if she ordered fries with that Whopper, you got to do that scene again. You got to be able to answer anything. Have people throw wrenches at it because you have to know.

The thing that I said to you last time that you were like, "Oh, I like that," was – if you don't know the exact answer to a question, you should know the world and the people enough…

SM: To create it right there…

AB: And it should be honest gospel and that will be that going forward. Yes, you got three kids? Just throw that out because three is a good number. You throw it out because you know that at three, she would stop doing anything.

SM: Right, good.

AB: …You know her enough to know it.

That thing with reality, you got to know these people enough to know – I always say there's two pitching meetings when it comes to talents with reality shows. There's a pitch meeting you have in front of them and there's a pitch meeting you have without them.

I sometimes ask people to leave talents outside and we talk first and then the talent comes in because there are some things you should be able to tell me that you don't want to say in front of them.

"She's a cry baby. She's got a big heart. She's a crybaby. She's going to cry every time whether she's happy or sad. She's a crying machine." So that whenever I ask her a question in the room, I'm probably going to try to get her to cry to see if that's true.

There are things about whether it's reality or script that you just have to know the world so much. You have to have told that story so much. The best stories around a campfire are the ones that are most vivid. The stories on podcasts are the ones you can actually see the leaves blowing on the tree because that person knows that world so well that they can tell you about it. Then lastly I would say, never forget that you're telling the story beyond the story that you're going to tell; always telling a lot of stories.

SM: When you're talking to the talent, how do they influence your decision? As far as the story is concerned, are you basically thinking, "I want to see how much of the creative story aligns with you?" What are you looking for in the conversation?

AB: I'm one of those people who kind of break the ice quickly. I share something in the room a little bit embarrassing about myself whenever there's talent. If *Sweetie Pie's* is in the room, I'm going to make myself a little foolish to make them a little more comfortable because network people intimidate these people.

I usually share something embarrassing about myself and then I say, and I say this in every pitching meeting, "Part of my job is I get to ask really personal, inappropriate questions about you. Are you ready?" And they always kind of laugh and they say, "Okay, let's go."

By that I'm admitting that what I'm about to ask might be uncomfortable, that you came in here to sell a show to me, so everything is on the table and I usually ask something really wild and crazy. Depending on the room and type of show that it is, I go edgy. I go edgy

---

· A reality television show that airs on the Oprah Winfrey Network and stars Robbie Montgomery.

110

as I can go. If it's a family show, I'll ask mom and dad who's their favorite kid with all the other kids in the room and watch their answer. That's about as edgy as I can go with a family.

With a couple it's like, "Is the sex still good?" If they have five kids, "Is the sex still good?" If you can't answer that, you shouldn't be doing TV. Also, it kind of sets the bar from them that "Look, I'm not an executive that's going to go away, I'm going to be involved personally."

They might read that as saying, "That was a great meeting. We'd love to be at BET but that was a little too personal. We're going with the VH1 offer." Everybody wins because what I don't need is for you come here and be shut down.

SM: It's good to know upfront.

AB: What you're really looking for in talent is their comfortability. It's probably a very stressful room, which means you're not only practicing the pitch, you're practicing with them to pitch several times with people they don't know.

I can tell when the talent has been prepped and when they haven't. Sometimes when they haven't, that's good. But you can prep them bad, "Don't say this. Don't mention that." You're sitting there playing them as wealthy people who live in this great suburb in Dallas and then I start talking to them and realize that, well you know, actually they're divorced and he lives in an apartment.

They weren't supposed to say that in the room. They will slip up. You got to trust your talent that they're going to be comfortable.

Most importantly, they have a point of view. I think a lot of times, people talk about what their arc type is, what they're like, right, "She's catty. She's the wealthy princess. She's the down and love-stricken one, blah, blah, blah." That's all really kind of great but the truth of the matter is, "Can I talk to this family of five people and in 15 minutes realize how different they all are? What's different about each of them?" If it's all Kumbaya, there's not going to be a show there. There's just not going to be a show there.

Then also, I have to feel that – one of the things that I love when talents are in the room is watching them watch the reel. Now, one of the worst things you can do is go into a room with a talent and show them what you're about to show somebody. You got that thing that happens and people get just shocked at the way they were portrayed.

But also seeing when they cringe, like if they have seen it a couple of times, they probably got some notes. If they cringe and they're like, "Gosh, I wish they'd have taken that part out." Okay, she doesn't like being portrayed as a bitch. That makes her cringe every time or look, she's seen this 10 times but holding her daughter still makes her cry.

It tells you a lot. Talent in the room tells you a lot. As a content creator, you really have to trust your talent. If you don't trust them, don't bring them.

SM: Right. As for Reality, what should one include in a pitch?

AB: This is a lot of different – you'll get a lot of different answers on this. For me, I am of the school that you never leave anything behind. You always follow up. There are a lot of reasons for that.

First of all, you can go into a room and you can pitch with only a paper treatment, a PowerPoint deck. You can do a full pilot presentation or sizzle reel, or you can do something in the middle which is sort of like you can create a piece of tape which is just Skype interviews and put photos and videos of people into it.

For me, those are the three main kinds – paper only, you pitch a finished product like a presentation or sizzle-reel, or you're pitching a casting tape. And, never leave anything in the room. I share it with you, I hear your feedback, and then I say, "You know what, let me tailor this and tweak it a little bit so it's perfect for you guys. I'll send it back in a couple of days."

The reason for that is I might have said to you in a room, "You know, we wished this was a female or we didn't like this one character." You can take them out and send something better for us.

Or if we say, "You know what, it would be great if this had a celebrity angle to it. You can go and include that stuff."

But the main reason I do it is from a networking and sales standpoint. You now have a reason to touch base with me next week and the other person doesn't. The other person is bothering me now whenever they check in to see what I thought about the pitch.

You were simply checking in to give me what you promised you were going to give me. But you get two chances to talk and that person gets one.

SM: That's smart. That's worth a million dollars.

AB: The worst thing in the world for content creators to do is to come across desperate, harassing or annoying to someone that you want to buy something from you. So often what you'll do is you'll submit your project and you might not hear for two months and after two months, then you're like, "Okay, maybe I should really check in."

Nobody really knows how long is good and how long is bad because it's person by person. Two months might be great at MTV. Two months here, I might have forgotten who you were...

SM: How do you gauge that?

AB: ...I might be, "Well, God. You didn't give me two weeks to share it with the team yet."

One of the things I feel like is we aren't very good; buyers aren't really good in this space either. We can be a little more proactive about how much time we need.

I try to do that. I try to say, "We'll have another development meeting in three weeks. If you haven't heard from me by then, feel free to reach back out." We manage feedback. I try to manage everything in my life. I try managing up, and I try to manage down. I try to manage sideways; manage my workflow response because I know I would reply within three weeks.

SM: Yeah but that means it's so subjective that there's really no answer from network to network how to follow up.

AB:	Here's the thing. The reason why what we do is one of the hardest things is because we use the left-brain and right brain. Sales are one of the hardest things to do and it's not a very creative way to sell; and it's not conducive to the creative process.

Here's the thing. The reason why what we do is one of the hardest things is because we use the left-brain and right brain. Sales are one of the hardest things to do and it's not a very creative way to sell; and it's not conducive to the creative process.

We create these things; they are our passions, they are our babies. But at the end of the day, we have to use the other side of our brain to actually sell them numbers wise, time wise. How many days are enough days?

It's the same reason you never know if you should call the guy back that night or wait three days. Nobody can still answer that question because it's subjective. It's on you to figure it out. It's on you to judge the room.

Somebody comes in and you're like, "Oh my God. I've been swamped this week. I've got so many pilots and presentations." Don't check back with them that week. Give them some time. (lol)

SM: Right, right.

AB: Somebody going on vacation, you wouldn't send it to them. You just got to learn how to read the room. Or if they say, "I don't know if this is good or bad but I'll be able to get a quick answer on this. Shoot me back in a couple of days." Go back in a couple of days. If they're saying what they mean, you can only assume they're saying what they mean.

It's one of the hard things about sales where it's up to you to judge each individual situation. That's why it's so important to network because if you pitch me a show more than twice, you know how long it's going to take me to get back.

SM: Let's say I have a pitch and it's something about it that you like. How does one prepare for the next steps? Because I know that that's something that we never really did, actually have that next meeting with you. But it always hung in my head, what would you have told me?

AB: The next step would have been budget and schedule. You guys would have to tell me how much that show is going to cost and how long it would take you under your plan to make it.

That could have been top line. You don't necessarily have to go hire a line producer to do it but it's got to be authentic. If you came back and say, "We can do it for $800,000 an episode." I'd say, "These people have no idea what we do." If you come back and say, "We can do it for $100,000 an episode," I'd say, "Oh that's a much cheaper looking show than I thought.

You got to be accurate there. That probably would have been the next step. The next step after that would be to do what's called a business affairs request. That's where we go to legal and say, "We want to make a contract with these people for this and here's what we want to do."

And more often than not, you would either do a development step, which is small and maybe on paper, or just find casting. Say it's a show about five publishers, and we want to find a publisher and do a casting step. Or it might be a small pilot like a presentation or pilot, or it might be straight to series.

So at that point, you're going to need somebody to negotiate on your behalf. That is the reason that most places will not take an unsolicited pitch. Because if we like your idea and we're ready to move on it, we don't have time for you to go find an attorney that we're going to deal with, who might not really be an attorney in this business.

If you have your agent, we call your agent. We can do that within a day.

SM: I'm so glad you told me that. I never knew what the big deal was about having an agent!

AB: People think it's to keep ideas out. It's not to keep ideas out; it's to make the deals.

SM: Oh my God, Austyn, do you understand how golden that information is? It's so good to know that.

AB: The main thing – no, you're right. The most deceiving thing in this business is you pitch some ideas and people won't hear them. And you are like, "I know I have a good idea and nobody will hear it."

You get defeated because you take that personal. "They don't think I'm good enough. I didn't graduate to college. I didn't go to Film School. I haven't written or made a great pilot."

115

It has nothing to do with that. It has to do with the amount of time it takes us to review. I mean, I get 1,200 pitches a year. Imagine if I did take unsolicited pitches from everyone, I'll have 4,200 pitches a year. My entire job will just be watching people's content.

It's to help us ink a deal. If you have it, if you're pitching before and you got an agent and the agent thinks that's great and we think it's great, that agent can do that deal in a day and so we'll deal with you even though you've never done anything.

I think the biggest thing is don't get personal, especially if you don't have an agent and nobody will take your pitch. It's not personal. It's the efficiency in which the deal has to be done.

And just because you've got a manager at a local strip mall to represent dancers and models, that's not the person who knows what a TV contract looks like. It's not in your best interest.

If you came to us without a lawyer, without an agent or without an attorney, we're going to make a deal with you but you wouldn't get anything. It wouldn't be in your best interest.

Most of the time, people have managers and associates and lawyers submit stuff on their behalf that really don't know the business. They're not going to be able to negotiate in their best interest anyway.

AB: Which could be years from now, and tie the show that we all made, up in litigation, because you didn't have the right agent. Now none of us get to do it again. It's all just to protect the deal.

SM: Yeah, I see now how that can become headache. I respect it now. I won't be so defeated by that. That makes a lot of sense. Wow.

One question I have is, "What are some of the things that will cause great ideas to get passed over?"

AB: We pass on most, or at least about 85% of the things we hear...I think the big thing with content creators and selling is don't take it personal. When I got to the network and realized why my shows didn't get the series – because I did a couple of pilots but they never went to series – I realized it had nothing to do with me. It had nothing to do with my show or me.

If you have the best show in television, people will make room for it and they won't make excuses. But a lot of times it's just, oh, they were interested in that but at the time we made it, TV viewership changed. It's ever-evolving.

If you have the best idea for television four years ago, it's probably not today. It could be the best idea for television again in two more years but it's not consistent.

We're always passing on things you love. We're sometimes picking up things that we're not thrilled to the roof about but you know there's something there and you want to develop it and see if 'there' is there.

Nothing is personal, unless it is, which you know...it will be personal. Like I said, you're always telling the story. If you're late to the meeting and you don't know the budget and you don't know your show, then yeah, it's probably always going to be personal for you.

But if you feel like you know your show, that you've got good shows and these networks are buying and these networks aren't. If you're selling shows, you're a good content creator. You can't let the "no's" bother you that much.

The thing that I think people don't do is – people always call me and ask for – and I would definitely include this somewhere. People always call me and ask for feedback on their show. You pitch a show to me and you follow up in a couple of weeks and you ask what we thought about it, people always do that.

I'm shocked at how many people follow up and ask for advice on how they pitched their show. We're eager to seek advice for our projects but we rarely seek advice about our own performance.

So the one thing I would say if you got back and forth with the network executive that you trust and you like and they seem knowledgeable and they seem friendly or at least helpful and not too busy, I'd follow up with them and say, "Hey, I'm sorry XYZ didn't work out for you. We'd love to come back and fix some other stuff. Thanks for sharing your mandate with us. Now, we really understand what you guys are looking for.

And by the way, I'm not sure if you noticed or not but I'm relatively new to pitching and wonder, did I leave a good impression or do you have anything that has to be worked on for my next pitch?"

I mean, I would remember that person. I would remember that person just because I don't get that phone call every day. And I would probably try to remember, if I don't remember you at all, I would say, "I don't really remember the pitch that well. I don't remember you that much to critique you."

That's not a good thing either. You still left a memorable impression in that meeting.

I think a lot of times, like I said, people are thick-skinned about their projects even to the point where they'll handle rejection or criticism, constructive criticism about our project but we don't think about ourselves and I think we should.

SM: I'm really glad you confirmed that.

AB: The other thing I think is I don't think people wrap enough after pitches. If you're pitching with a partner, you guys should stop after that pitch and talk. Did we like what happened in there? What can we change next time?

SM: I agree. I value all you have to say.

AB: That's great. I just want to be helpful.

SM: You are. It's great information to know.

Christopher Nolen

President of Nferno Productions

As President of Nferno Productions, the production company he founded in 1998, Christopher Nolen has created a proven brand in urban entertainment, production, and distribution by creating positive and entertaining content for minorities and global audiences as a whole. As a Director, Nolen's projects under Nferno Productions include the feature-length films *Deep Passion, Subtle Seduction, The Good Life, Four Seasons,* and the recently completed *72 Hours.* On January 16, 2014, Nolen's film *The Good Life* made its network debut after being acquired by BET (Black Entertainment Television). The film received such stellar ratings and reviews that it continues to have a recurring monthly slot on the network's schedule. *The Good Life* was originally released nationwide on July 16, 2013. Nolen, and stars Tangi Miller, Chicago's very own, Richard Gallion, Christian Keyes, Maya Gilbert, and Mari Morrow. He had another nationwide release on April 1, 2014 of his film, *Four Seasons,* which he wrote, produced, and directed. The film stars Robin Givens, Keith Robinson, Christian Keyes, Jazsmin Lewis, and Chicago's own Mel Jackson. "Four Seasons" was shot entirely in Chicago in July of 2013. Nolen is currently in post-production with his latest and most highly anticipated film *72 Hours,* which features an amazing star-studded ensemble cast, including Chicago's own Timon Kyle Durrett of *VH1's Single Ladies,* Erica Hubbard of BET's *Let's Stay Together,* and legendary star and acting sensation, Harry J. Lennix, of NBC's #1 show *The Black List.* Rounding out the cast is Terri J. Vaughn of *The Steve Harvey Show,* Brian Hooks of the TV series *Eve,* Cynda Williams of *Mo Betta Blues,* Tangi Miller of *Felicity,* Brely Evans of BET's *Being Mary Jane,* and Chyna Layne of *Precious.* Nolen is also in development on two new exciting feature-length films entitled "Zodiac Sign" and "Lustful Decisions." He is excited and passionate about writing, directing and producing films and is looking to expand those talents into the world of television. Nolen graduated from the University of Illinois at Urbana, Champaign in Electrical Engineering with a minor in Theatre.

SM: Talk about packaging your projects. How do you go about packaging your projects?

CN: Great question. First thing of course is start with the script. If I write a script or if I get a script from a writer, it

119

has to be a story that fits my brand. If I have a good product the first thing I do is talk with my casting director and we go over the script, go over characters, and then go over names that will fit the character's story. Then, we also go over names that investors and distributors would want in this film so they can pick up the film to distribute it. That's key.

I do that with my casting director and producers. What my cast director does there, because this is also his project, he will go ahead and call some of the actors directly or he might call the agents and managers and that he has relationships with directly as well. Because the key when packaging your film is getting talent so you can get the financing that you need to make the film.

So, I would tell anybody to start with the script and also either hire a casting director or ask a producer for their actors and their agency directly. Once you get those actors that you want, then you start going to investors and begging them for money.

SM: What about the independent filmmaker? Can you think back to some of your earlier films when you maybe didn't always have a casting director? Or did that become the thing to do, getting a casting director to tap into the type of actors that you want?

CN: When I started with the couple of films back in the late 90s, early 2000s, the industry was different then, so you could make a film back then with up-and-comers on the movie. I pretty much knew the actors that I wanted to work with, we were all up-and-coming in the industry. It's so funny, I started off an actor as a child and I went behind the camera after I graduated from college. So I knew people.

Then, it was just easy to call up the actors that you work with in the past commercials, and videos with and say, "I want you as an actor in this movie." That's changed these days. These days, as a producer or a director, you either have to have those contacts, or you hire a casting director, or another producer that might have those contacts to get the talent that you need and that's going to garner a distribution deal and finance it.

My suggestion for up-and-coming directors and producers, if you want to get money to your projects and make them quality, then you're going to need a Hollywood talent to do that because the investors, they want their money back. If you do this film without Hollywood talent, it's going to be tough these days to get distribution. It's going to be tough for a distributor to want to give money for a project that they can't promote or sell.

SM: That makes a lot of sense. Could you elaborate on what that means for an independent content creator, especially a novice?

CN: So for the first timer, I'm going to suggest that you do it for as cheap as possible. You invest in the project yourself. That's what I always tell people.

Invest in yourself. Take the money from your savings account and make your first feature film if you can. Short films are good. I call them mini-resumes. But if you are going to spend any money on something, you want to make a feature-length film, which is over 60 minutes long, generally; most networks or distributors want the film over 75 minutes. But if you do that, shoot for a cheap as possible. Get some up-and-comers. But the story has got to be amazing so then you get a better look when you start putting it in film festivals.

I think for novices, film festivals are great because now you have a different audience coming to see your film.

I always say that if you're shooting and are a first-time filmmaker/director/producer, get some good up-and-coming talent that can actually be believable on the screen for you. The only way you're going to get any other money is if you sell or show other people that you've invested in yourself.

SM: That's great information. I also want to talk about your process. So the process is to get a great script, whether you've written it or you are executive producing the script, and then find a talent with your casting director. You create a wish list and you talk about who can do it from either the wish list or based upon your or the casting director's network.

And then, seek money, investors. Right?

CN: Yes. Investors, the first question they're going to ask…

121

SM: Who do you have in it?

CN: Who is in it? Who's in the movie? Because I want to invest thousands in the movie, I want to have a greater chance to get my money back. That means it's got to be someone that the world knows so they will pick up the movie.

SM: It's a catch-22 because investors want to know who's in your film, and actors want to know how much they're getting paid. But, if you don't have the money invested, you can't quite answer that. How do you get around that?

CN: Relationships. Relationship is key. I tell all filmmakers, directors and producers, you got to rub elbows with these actors. And the actors should also want to rub elbows with directors and producers. Everybody should be working together cohesively as a team these days especially if it's independent.

I do understand that people have to eat; they have rent, or mortgage. I get that. But sometimes there's just a special project out there that you got to just do for the love. I always tell my friends that are actors to have a rate for studio or network projects. I mean they have a decent rate for independents that makes the independent world better if we know that there's a certain rate that we can get an actor for in an independent project.

You're not going to make money doing independent projects. It's just not in the cards these days. Ask anybody. You're basically doing the projects because they tell great stories. Passionate stories. Build your resume. Build your films.

SM: Or maybe if an actor is tired of being typecast and are like, "I need to change my world and this is a great script to do that."

CN: Absolutely. The catch-22 is very accurate. But I think it's the relationship and both parties are comfortable, get it to work. I worked with so many great Hollywood talents, talented actors. They really came on board not just for the scripts and the story. The actors really came because we have relationships with each other.

SM: If you can go back to the early 90s or early 2000s, before you had these relationships with these Hollywood actors, how did you connect with them?

CN: That's a great question. Just being at networking events such as film festivals. That's a great place where you can network with actors. Actors are in film festivals because they either have a movie that's being shown that they're starring in or they might also have produced. When you're there at film festivals, networking events around the world, you rub shoulders with them. You talk to them directly. You build relationships with them.

For me also, I was able to develop relationships with some of these actors because they'd heard of my name and me just from working. Filmmakers must get out there at these events and get to know these actors, directors, or producers.

It's almost like when you're pledging a fraternity or sorority. You got to get to know those brothers or sisters that's in that fraternity or sorority that you want to pledge. You got to get to know them and they got to get to know you so they can feel comfortable with you to bring anyone in to that fraternity or sorority.

Filmmaking is the same thing. You got to get out there to get to know those people in a legal manner. Notice that I used the word "legal" because there are crazy people these days. You got to put yourself in their position. Somebody you might know, they might know Morris Chestnut. That happens. You just go into that environment and that event or whatever and try to meet him and make an impression on him in that situation.

That's how I think you can get started. Just going to these events. Going to these film festivals and rubbing elbows and shoulders with people, if they're very passionate with what you're trying to do.

You can use another one, Squeaky. Get with other producers and directors who work in this industry, go on their sets and be an intern. Learn from them. Seek them out as a production assistant so you can then start developing those relationships as well. Does that make sense?

SM: Makes a lot of sense. That's great advice.

CN: That's where you can really get to know their community. Being a production assistant, you work closely with the producers on the set and sometimes you can be a personal assistant for a star actor and meet directors. From there, you don't worry about what you do. You soak up that knowledge and the experience. When you have that script that you want to do and you've done a great job on the director/producer's set, you can say, "Hey I think I'm ready to do this script. Will you take it and read it?" And I'll say, "You did a great job for me, I got it."

SM: How much talent do you seek out before you go to the investor?

CN: You ask such really great questions. It just depends. If I've got a real big name that I think everybody knows, I think I'll just use one. But I personally love to do ensemble casts. I love ensemble casts where I can get a group of four, five, or six actors that all have relevant credits in the business and names and we get together. I want to package them that way as well. Either-or, it's just the same.

To get investors on board, I always have to prove to them that I'm on board with my own money, my credit cards, and my savings account. When they see that, they take me more seriously.

SM: Do you have a look book when you go in to investors?

CN: Yes, absolutely. I do. I think the look book just puts you in a better position when you're asking for an investor to invest in your film. Some say film investing is risky. But I say any investment is a risk – stocks, bonds, and real estate. It's the same thing for me. But you have all your ducks in a row in a look book and it's very presentable and you have a credible producer that's got movies distributed or a viable actor, I think an investor will be open to investing in the project especially if he or she wants to get into the industry like that. I invest in every film that I do.

SM: How do you determine how much you will invest in your own work? What happens when investors learn that you've invested your own funds?

CN: Being a former math teacher, I like to make the math for investors as easy as possible. I show them a bank account for the production, "This is my money. This is for Christopher Nolan. I'm putting up half of the budget. I'm asking you to match my half and we will be partners in this production."

SM: By saying the word "partner," they feel kind of wholesome about that. I'm very personable with my investors. Do you know what I mean?

SM: That's so valuable: certain words are key, "partner." It says if he's willing to take a risk on his own money, then I'm not as afraid because half of his money is up.

CN: They think, "He's putting up half his money. He's about to go in debt to make this movie and we're about to be partners. All right, I got to go in. I got to be in this film." That's what it is to me. It's that word "partners" and it's that communication with those investors that they believe. Because there have been some shady people in this industry, Squeaky, that have run off with money and it's hurting us as filmmakers because those investors who have the money have heard horror stories about it.

A person like myself coming from a genuine heart, genuine place and wanting partners to come on board with the project is very key. I think asking them to be a partner of the project makes them want to at least take a hard look at it. Of course they're going to ask, "How much have your other films made?" Things of that sort. You have to be upfront with them. You just tell them, "We started with this amount of money. We got this amount of money back." It made profit or we broke even. And if you are as honest as possible with them then hopefully they will say yes. Not only will they say yes, they will have a certified check for you to go cash into the bank account.

SM: When you first started seeking out investors, did you always provide half or did you ask for all of the money? What did you do then when you didn't have half of 250,000 or whatever the budget was for your film? How did you go half? What did you ask for? What was that process like? How did you get that investor and secure the deal?

CN: I did it a little different than that on my earlier films. I financed my early films pretty much on my own. And then, my immediate family came on board to invest as well. So it was the Nolan family that invested in my first film or two.

Once I got those films done and my name started to get out there, I needed to get more money to make…

125

SM: Better quality, bigger films...

CN: Luckily, my name is out there and I had a pretty good resume. My film got distributed and it was myself and my family members to come on board to invest and I was able to go meet with people within real estate. Those were my first investors that bought into the Nolan family; real estate investors.

SM: You're the second or third person that put me on to real estate investors.

CN: The real estate investors who are flipping houses and making 30, 50, 60 or 70,000 on each house, cash money. If I know they're doing that, can you do 25,000 my way on this project? I already have 50,000 in myself. If you can get 25,000, can you refer another person that you know who will be willing to do that as well?

It was like a chain. Once I get that one investor to invest and believe, I ask them to refer other people.

SM: You said a lot in these 28 minutes that is incredibly helpful, but those three things are so valuable because it's the independent way. No, that's not the independent way. Screw that. That's beyond independent. That's the smart business way. That's Hollywood. It's just on a smaller level but it's what they're doing.

CN: Absolutely. It's a situation where if you get that one "yes," that person that believes and they believe in you. You say, "Look, can you get some other people to believe in *you*?" It's a chain affect.

I've been lucky to get other people to invest in me. I really have. It's still hard. It's tough because once you get the investors their money back either they like to re-invest in the next project or they might take their money and go back to real estate or invest in some other things. It just depends on the investor.

But I've been really lucky to get into a situation where I can actually invest in myself. I think knowing one actually well, it's really helpful. It's helped me tremendously.

SM: That's another question. How do you repay these investors? Are they getting what they invested back plus a certain amount? What does that look like?

CN: That's a good question and I can answer it. It depends on the investor. Generally, when you ask an investor for money, you want to give them at least, in my opinion, 10% return on their investment. If somebody invests $10,000, you want to give him or her back $1,000. Some investors might say, "Hey, I need more than that."

So it's up to you as a producer if you want to give more than 10%. If you don't want to give more than 10% then you just walk away from that potential money. But if you're willing to give more than 10%, that's your decision. It just depends on what you want to do, how you want to structure everything financially.

SM: Do you generally look for the money yourself or do you get brokers or consultant, and EPs involved to look for money as well?

CN: I would like to do it myself so I really know the business, but if I can find other executive producers or brokers to find an investor that is great too. And generally, what happen with brokers is if they find financing, they want a finder's fee. I'm cool with that. That makes sense. Everybody pays for relationships in the real world. That's real. In the real world, you got to pay for relationships because everybody has to eat.

I definitely have been lucky and I would tell novices to start using your own money, and then tap into your family, and then tap into your friends. See who is down for the calls right now. You're trying to make a movie and you're a first timer, let's see who I can call. Let me call my family, let me hit my friends up, my sorority or fraternity brothers up and see who is down. Because, if they're down for you early, then you definitely know they're going to be down for you later in the game.

SM: A filmmaker, Antoine Allen, told me the same profound information. He said, "As far as investment goes, you start in your own backyard. Period. We always go for these big conglomerates, and big names. We're going for Coca-Cola and all of the big time executive producers but don't go for the most known name or person. Don't go for the person that everybody is vying for." He reminded me of Will Packer and Rob Hardy and how they went to Bronner Brothers.

CN: Yeah, absolutely.

SM: As far as a casting director is concerned, if you don't have money, how do you get them on board?

127

CN: Squeaky if you were a casting director and I knew you could get certain actors I would say, "Squeaky, alright, I really love your work. I really love what you have casted in the past. I want to work with you. I don't have any money, but I want to bring you on board as a producer, as a partner, with me on this project." Hopefully you can use your relationships to get these actors because if we can get actors, then we will be able to get financing for this film.

Or the finances for this film might not be a lot but we'll get some more money back when the movie is done. If that's the case, then you go and get your money that way. Once there is a profit, then boom! There it is. Either she is down for the cause or not.

I get it that everybody needs to work and make money. But if the project and the script are good and the casting director believes in it, and believes in you as the producer/director, they'll know it. Everybody needs to add to his or her resume. That's real talk.

SM: Right. That's true.

CN: Everybody needs to add to his or her resume. You can say it's a good quality film, which has great potential to get to distribution.

SM: I like that. "Everybody needs to add to their resume." That's quotable.

SM: My last question to you is, "How did you go about getting distribution?"

CN: What happened when I got my first film distributed, I had a trailer for the film and it was getting played at every film festival; I had put it in several film festivals. Then the acquisitions person from a distribution company saw it and said, "I want your movie." Now, I'm young and excited for it to get picked up. I thought about submitting it, and thought, let me talk to an entertainment attorney.

That's something that filmmakers need to have. They need to have an entertainment attorney in their camp because their entertainment attorney represents them, represents the project, and he or she will let that filmmaker know if that's a good deal or not.

The film festivals helped me get me my first distribution deal way back then. They also help today as well,

SM: especially if they don't have a lot of Hollywood talent in their films.

SM: Now, do you get distribution in the front end or the back end of the film? In other words, do you go straight to the distribution company and say, "I have not shot this film yet, but these are the talents. I want to know if I can do a deal now?"

Do you negotiate it like that or do you wait until it's already in the can to try to get them the distribution deal?

CN: Great question. You have to lead the way. For me I can get a cast together who I want to use who I think will be very viable for distribution. What I will do is, I will call my sales agents and say, "This is what I have. Do you know of any networks, distributors, or studios alike who will also like to be a part of this film once it is done?" He'll search for that and say I can see if I get a couple of people that might be interested.

They don't give you the money for it; they have to see the final product. What they will do is they will give a letter of intent stating that based on the cast and the production quality of this film we are really interested now in seeking distribution for this film. That's good.

Or you can shoot the film, make it look great, sound great and then shop around after you finished everything with it.

SM: Yeah, I got that down.

CN: That's another key element of packaging because sales agents have their relationships with the distributors, or the networks to pick up the film. Generally, sales agents charge a fee between 15% and 30% – could be more depending on who the selling agent is, but they charge a fee. Whatever they get your film sold for, they take it out of that. That makes them want to work hard because they want to get paid. If they find a distributor that's going to pick up your film for a million dollars and they can get 15% of that, then they are doing pretty well.

It can work either way. You turn it in at the beginning or the end as far as getting distribution. It usually works when you are finished shooting because there's a lot of distributors who do not want to distribute anything because what if the movie never gets made.

SM: That makes sense. Well, that's all the questions that I have. You really spelled out the process so well.

129

Endyia Kinney-Sterns

Former Vice President of Programming and Development at OWN

Kinney-Sterns, recently named one of the Top Female Executives in Hollywood by *Essence Magazine*, has been instrumental in identifying and developing various new programming in her VP of Development & Programming role at OWN, including the popular docu-series *Raising Whitley* and ratings hit *Deion's Family Playbook* with Edmonds Entertainment and Lionsgate, and was an integral part in developing the hit show *Flex and Shanice* in addition to many presentations and pilots.

An accomplished television producer and executive for over 15 years, Kinney-Sterns has produced shows for high-profile networks including VH1, CBS, NBC, HGTV and production companies such as Buena Vista Television, Arnold Shapiro Productions and LMNO. As an executive at TV ONE, she was responsible for the day-to-day supervision of production and programming for popular series including *Baisden After Dark*, *Who's Got Jokes* and *Black and Men Revealed*. Her most notable accomplishment was co-developing and creating the brand defining, multiple NAACP Award winning hit show *Unsung*.

Kinney-Sterns spent over four years working in programming and development at BET where she was responsible for overseeing production and post production for the network's top-rated series *College Hill* and the highest rated show in BET history at the time, *Keyshia Cole: The Way It Is*. She was also responsible for helping to develop, launch, and oversee the day-to-day production of *The Mo'Nique Show*, the #1 late night talk show among African Americans as well as the hit music competition show *Sunday Best* and other ratings hits like, *Lil Kim: Countdown to Lockdown*, and *DMX, Soul of a Man*. Prior to her positions at BET and TV ONE, Kinney-Sterns produced reality, talk/variety and lifestyle shows including the Emmy Award-winning syndicated series *The Wayne Brady Show*, *Big Brother 4* and *The Other Half* among others.

SM: I learned that you created an animation that was picked up and you also started your own production company. I would like to talk about your process and how you went about getting that picked up. When it was picked up, you weren't well-known at that time?

131

EKS:	Not at all. It was an option. Which means it never really got made. But the idea was taken off the table to try to develop. The truth is people will option your idea if they like it, but if regime changes or partner changes happen it like fall to the wayside. It's like being shelved. Do you know what I mean? That's what happened to it.
	I will tell you, how I got through was I had a friend who knew someone –I was a producer at that time so I made a lot of connections, had some relationships and I had been around, not a long time but just enough to where people would say "She's creative, I trust to connect her to someone I know and get her in the room." That's what happened.
	I came from VH1. That was my feet in the water. Prior to that it was Edmonds Entertainment. I'd interned and then I became an associate story editor on *Soul Food*, ShowTime Show and then I got a job at VH1. It was a Viacom network. So I had relationships with all the people from the Viacom entities, from Nickelodeon, to MTV, to all of them just by working at VH1 for so long.
	I just tapped in to my pool of resources once I had this idea that I thought would be great for Nickelodeon. They then connected me to the development director there who gave me time.
SM:	Interesting enough, I worked for Viacom for three years. I just stopped in September. Initially I did the same thing. I was like, "You know what. I'm here. I need to use these resources." I was a bit afraid of it at first but then I started reaching out and I pitched Nickelodeon and they asked for the script but they ended up passing on it.
	The development executive was really helpful with advising me on how to establish where my show needed to be, and not to dumb it down to anybody but to put in its rightful place.
EKS:	All of that matters.
SM:	Yeah. You said you "asked." You know, so many people don't believe in the power of just asking. I could say that until I'm blue in the face and people will say, "How did you get that meeting?" And I'd say,

132

"Well, I asked someone to ask someone to do a soft introduction." They'd say, "Come on. That's not what did it." And I'm like, "Yes, it really is."

Because as an independent content creator without representation, people are always trying to figure out, how I get through these barriers without representation. Well, you may not remember it. I reached out to you maybe a few years ago, right before *The Have and Have Nots* was set to air; it was in development at the time, but I reached out to pitch a drama and you said at that time that you were only taking Tyler's [Perry's] projects.

But how does that work? With OWN network, do we have to have representation to get meetings with you?

EKS: Yes. Unless you have a pre-existing relationship or you're coming through someone who knows someone. Otherwise what ends up happening is you get people who aren't as well-versed as you in the industry and they come and they pitch, and you think you're doing something nice, but because they don't understand the way the business works, they'll turn to me a month later and see something similar with theirs and they come after me.

SM: I get it.

EKS: It's a problem. I have been put in that position. It's very strict now because anybody and everybody can sue. It's a serious situation when you're dealing with a high profile network such as OWN with someone at the helm. It's times 20 compared to other networks that I've been at. Because on the one end, they don't like turning people away, on the other end there's a lot of space because it's not an entity, it's a person and entity.

I think OWN is doubly harder. What's cool is we're one of the only networks that do have an unsolicited pitch process where you can go online and pitch your idea and they do get read every day. If something is there that works then we will reach out. A lot of other networks will never give you that opportunity.

.

133

| SM: | I think that is so amazing. That's good to know. Everyone's network and studio should have that option. |
| EKS: | You know what's so unfortunate though, and here's the bottom line, nobody really thinks about the business aspect of it ever. Put yourself in my position. Somebody comes to you with a great idea, right? And that great idea, who's going to make it? Who's going to develop it? You don't have the experience; you don't know how to execute it, who's going to do it? Then I have to take the time to do your job. The key is, if you know the business and you've done your homework, you should know that hiring a production company who's going to come in the door with their agent, it's already packaged, the deal's already done, you've got somebody who believes in your idea because it's a good idea. They've vetted it. They've helped you develop it. You bring it in the door and it's done. |

The thing is you may not get all the credit. You may have to share it. You may not get all the money that you think you should, but the thing is, it gets you through the door and it gives you an opportunity.

It's not that people, you know, it's so hard to get to the door because even when you get to the door there's still work to be done. It's just difficult because everyone has great ideas.

By the time you come over with an unscripted idea, I guarantee 3 other people have come over with the same idea and they probably pitch it 20 times. But the person, I know, it's sad, but it's the truth. The idea that gets bought is the idea that's packaged. Literally, I was pitched the same idea two weeks in a row and I bought that idea because they had talent attached and a production company already attached. That's the idea that gets bought.

| SM: | I guess takeaway is if you want to get through the door, see if you can go to a production company who has a relationship with OWN, or whatever network you're looking to go to, and see if they'll pick it up and help develop it. |

EKS: That's something else, too. A lot of times people don't do their homework even thinking about where your idea can fit.

Here's the deal. This is what I tell people. There are two types of ideas. There's the idea that's a passion and there's the idea that is marketable. 100% of the time a passion idea is not marketable. It could only fit one place. You put your heart and soul into it and you got to be okay with if that one place that will suit your show passes on it, you're okay because that's your passion and you gave it your best shot.

Because people don't want to think. If you're going to do an idea, you can't just do an idea just for you. You think you have an idea then you have to think supply and demand. If this idea works and you're putting money, time in or anybody else because then you'll be able to pitch to as many people as possible to get a better opportunity to sell it.

If you have an idea that only fit a Fuse or OWN, well the production company knows based on what their agents and managers tell them, their relationship with me, they know, OWN is only looking for one specific thing because they have one hole a year and a half from now.

That is why it's important to have an agent or come with a production company because I'm not just going to scour unsolicited submissions portal looking for that great idea because even if it's a good idea, who's going to do it number one? Number two, because the likelihood of it being what I need is one in a million, one in a gazillion. A production company will know because we have talks, they're reaching me every week, they're emailing me. I talk to them every day all day. They know exactly what I need.

SM: How easy is it for a random person to call and say, "I'm just calling to find out what your mandate is, what type of shows you are looking for?"

EKS: That's not going to happen because I don't have time for that. What you do is you Google. You Google and you look and see, "Wow, this is upfront. This is the direction." Really look at my programming. Look at what I just bought. Look at what I am airing. Listen to what's being said about the direction of the network and what they just picked up. It's all out there. Just do your homework.

SM: You're right about that. What's the difference between a good and a great pitch? How do you determine which [pitch] is the one?

EKS: I have a checklist of what I want. A good pitch to me is someone coming in and knowing exactly what I want, what I'm doing, and what I don't want. They've done their homework, they know what I need and they pitch it to me.

For example, I'm looking for a celebrity ensemble family-driven docu-series. My core view is an African-American woman on Saturday night. They'll come in the room and say, "I have the best celebrity-driven ensemble docu-series." Usually when you get in the room, I need a logline, I need to know what it is. I won't even take the meeting unless I know it's worth it because I don't want to waste anyone's time.

If it's made, to me it means there's something intriguing about. So when they get into the room, they can sell it. They got to set it up properly. They got to let me know "Listen. it gives you all the things you want, with celebrity, and drama," and it's how they know exactly where the story is going to go. They know exactly where the characters are and the depth and breadth of their characters. They know the beginning, middle, and end of the story. They've broken down what I'm going to ask to see for each episode potentially. They know exactly what it takes to do a show pitch and what is required. I expect to get that in the room.

SM: Okay. You said so much great stuff without me having to ask. I really appreciate that. What is the likelihood of OWN optioning a great concept that isn't developed or packaged with talent? Does that ever happen where you're like, they haven't packaged it at all but it's just really a good idea.

EKS: No, no way. You understand, right? The only way is if they have a celebrity. It's disappointing but I get emails saying, "Oh my god, I have this great idea with Serena." I'm like, okay what's the idea? "She's going

136

	to open up a shop." Okay, she's opening up a shop. Who are the people? What's the story? What's the story arch? Who's going to shoot it? Who's going to produce it?
SM:	Do you mind if people come in with just a paper pitch without a sizzle?
EKS:	No. It's pointless. Why would I do that?
	I'm not going to give you $3 million based on paper – and it's a character driven show. No way!
	Other places might. They might be able to take a swing. I know some people who are just hard up for programming, they'd give you money to shoot that thing if you've got a talent attached and it's a world that they're looking for. That could work. But I'm in a position where I'm not hard up for programming. I'm going to need to see who are the people you are talking about.
	If you're pitching a docu-series that's character driven, paper is not going to do it. I have not seen any network that's like, "Oh my god, on paper you're great." No. They're going to want to see something. Skype, tape, something.
SM:	Endyia you've been great. I don't have any more questions because you're so thorough in your answers and just so straightforward. You were so helpful.

Eddie Harris
Writer – *Producer*

Eddie Harris was born on June 3, 1972 in Jersey City, New Jersey. Eddie's father, a former actor, was a consummate storyteller and the person Eddie credits with nurturing his early appreciation of the arts.
After studying Drama and Communications at Trenton State College in Trenton, New Jersey, Eddie began working at The A Group, a commercial and music video production company. At The A Group. Eddie learned the art of film making and directing. A random meeting with Ray Murphy, President of Eddie Murphy Productions, quickly turned Eddie's focus from directing to screenwriting after Eddie got a chance to read the script for *Nutty Professor 2*. With his astuteness, passion and hunger to learn, Eddie has gone on to write over fifty screen plays for films of different genres, including romance, comedy, horror, and sci-fi.
Now a more seasoned writer, Eddie has worked as a freelance writer in the film industry on various projects for many years. Eddie wrote the screenplay for, *"House Of Bodies."* This horror film produced by Queen Latifah's, Flavor Unit Productions, stars Oscar nominees Queen Latifah and Terrence Howard and Oscar Winner Peter Fonda.
Most recently, Eddie wrote the screenplay for the film, *"Zoo,"* that he also produced. *"Zoo"* is a drama based on the notorious New Jersey Zoo Crew starring Jermaine Hopkins (Juice) and J.D. Williams (HBO's *The Wire).*
Eddie has created, written and produced a television series comedy entitled "*Laid*". "*Laid*" can best be described as the "unorthodox" male version of *Sex In the City*, He has also written the motion picture screenplay.
Eddie also wrote the screenplay for, *"Robbery."* This drama/thriller, which is also produced by Flavor Unit Productions, and stars Terrence Howard and Mekhi Phifer. Currently in production.
Eddie is the director, writer and producer for the documentary "*Flip*". "*Flip*" is the true story of a kid from the inner city who went from street flipping to going on to become the 11-Time World Champion of Power Tumbling and numerous film and television appearances.
Eddie strives to create film and television projects through his film

SM: Tell me how you got started.
EH: Writer and producer. My strongest area is writing. I got into the business actually to be a director. I wanted to be a music video director during the days when record labels

138

were paying 6-7 digits checks to do music videos. I was a big Hype Williams fan. That era. I left College after two years to come back to Jersey to work for a commercial and lease video company called the Eight Group based in Manhattan. Didn't get paid just did an internship. It was commercial and music video internship. I wanted to learn how to basically make music videos. I learned by watching by being a PA how videos were made. I took that knowledge back to my hood and started doing local videos for local rappers for no money or on shoestring budgets. That's when I kind of realized I didn't like the headaches of directing. So, I had a friend that worked with Marvel comics and I approached him one day and said, "Listen, I have an idea. I want you to draw out the characters and then I'll write a story for them." The idea was taking 30 NBA players and making them into little kids. So we had Shaq, Dennis Rodman, and all these different ball players, and Lisa Leslie from WNBA as kids. He drew these amazing characters that jumped out of the page. I wrote a story about these characters that were friends and their relationships and it landed on the desk of Ray Murphy at Eddie Murphy Enterprise in New York. They brought me in and I optioned it. That's when I started to learn the process of development and TV show animation. While I was there, I used to commute back and forth from Jersey to New York and I would go through the Village and see this guy outside named Vlady; selling movie scripts. I would never understand why, used to think "Why would people just go buy scripts when they could just go watch the movie?" I had no idea the importance of that.

One day I'm in Ray's office, and he's going to lunch and I saw the script for *Nutty Professor 2*. It was my first time actually picking up a script to read. I was excited because it was *Nutty Professor 2*, and the movie wasn't shot yet. I asked him if I could read it and he said, "Sure." When he went to lunch I read the script and was amazed. I connected with the way the script was written, the flow, the words, the format; everything. I couldn't put it down. When Ray came back from lunch, he asked if I'd read it and I said yes! I was excited. I said, "I can't wait to see the movie." He says, "Yeah, well we'll get to it." So I said, "Well, what did you think about the script?" He said, "It was okay." So I asked, "Well what did Eddie think about the script?" He goes, "Eddie hated it. He ripped it up and he's hiring a writer. This is the 6th writer that we had to hire." That's when I learned that writing goes through different rewrites, different writers, before it comes to the final draft.

I say, "Wow. Man, Eddie didn't like it? What did you have to pay this guy?" He says, "We had to pay them all 1.5 million dollars." So I asked, "He had to give all that money back?" And he goes, "No, we had to pay him all of that upfront."

At that point right there, all I could think is, "Damn, writers get paid that much money?"

SM: Ha! You were hooked.

EH: I was hooked! I said, "Okay, I need to learn how to write. Now, I failed English in high school and college. I wasn't interested in writing. But when I read this script it was something that just clicked. I connected with the script.

I immediately left that office and went back to that guy Vlady down by NYU and I started buying his scripts. I bought *Scarface*, *The Mummy*, all of these different scripts, all different genres..." Let me get a Horror, let me get an Action, a Comedy. I would just buy all these scripts. He was selling them for $10. I bought $100 worth of scripts. So, I shot home and I started reading them. I read them all and would keep reading them over. I didn't realize that I was reading the final drafts of the scripts. Vlady's friend would take the scripts, because the movie studio would throw them away after they finished shooting the movie. His friend would pick up the script, send them back to Vlady, and Vlady would make copies and would sell them.

So, I'm reading the final draft of scripts that had been through several writers' hands. I learned the formats and style of writing, not knowing that I was subconsciously teaching myself. Finally, I had saved up enough money to get final draft program. I think it was like $400. During that time, I had an idea that I wanted to write. I would take notes and walk around with all these sheets of paper, waiting until I got the final draft program. Once I got it Squeaky, I sat down and I wrote that script in a day.

I would not stop until I flushed that idea out. I had so many notes, and scenes and dialogue. Once I flushed it out I was so excited. But as I'm writing it, I was so consumed and focused on it that I begin to like create dialogue and build characters. It wasn't a good story when I look back on it, but I got it out. It was like a high writing. I immediately started writing another one. I said, "I flushed that one out in a day, I'm going to try to flush this one out in one day too." And I flushed out my 2nd story. I had written 90 pages for the first and 108 pages for the second one. This was my introduction to the world of writing.

At that time, there were a lot of rappers that were trying to get into the film world. Because I had a relationship with Flavor Unit, Latifah's company, I had access to a lot of these rappers. I was able to convince one of these rappers to let me write their script. From that point on, I just took off. I used that job to pretty much help me get the next job from another rapper. Then there was just a snowball effect. Back then, when writing for rappers, the scripts weren't all that great. They just told a typical story, the struggle and the hood. I became a master at writing those kinds of stories. My name started floating around in the industry as that go-to guy to write your script. That's where it all started.

As things with Flavor Unit started to progress, and they started to get into the film world, then I had to step my game up. I started reading scripts that were outside the box like *Star Wars*, Sci-fi, and Horrors. So I would go to this guy Vlady and get these scripts and read them so I could be familiar with how those types of scripts read. It just became a love. I started to mix and mingle with other creative people and look at their work, see how they would develop and create things. I began building relationships and would bounce ideas around with other people. Then I started stepping out, I'd say, "I think I'm going to wrote a Romantic Comedy…" and that's how it all started. That was like 20 years ago.

SM: I know by now you've written many scripts and have done quite a bit in the industry. How did you attach people to your projects?

EH: Some of it was through relationships, by being

141

introduced or walked through the door under someone's wing. Other times, it was me going directly to talent, getting to them by other means. Whether it was through a friend or business associate. I was constantly in their faces, or in their emails, or on their phone by a text or call. And it was really me going after them and getting them to read something of mine.

SM: Could you tell me your step-by-step process? You don't have to name drop. But if you could tell a specific story about getting someone to read your script, that would be helpful to the reader.

EH: I have a few stories. In one story, I had a relationship with a guy who did films at a production company. They knew me because I would write scripts from different genres and I would take little snippets and I would print out the snippets. I would say, "Here are 2-3 pages from an Action movie, a Comedy, from a Sci-fi and I would give it to them and let them see like, "Oh this guy can write a bunch of different genres." So one day, one of the guys, actually I'm cool with him now, I'm very big on relationships in the business because that's what helps you a lot. So the guy calls me in the office one day and says, "Listen, we got this idea for a movie that we want to do, and here it is." He gives me a sheet of paper that's literally a paragraph.

SM: A concept.

EH: And I'm like, "This is what y'all are doing the movie on? And he says, "Yeah." So, he says, "Can you write the script?" And I say, "I'll write a 20-page teaser based off of this and I'll get it to y'all." He says, "Cool." So I write the 20-page teaser and get it to him. He reads it. He cracks up, and gives it to his boss. I get a call maybe two weeks later from his boss in LA, and he goes, "Congratulations." I say, "What's up?" And He says, "I just gave Columbia the 20-page teaser based on the idea of the movie we want to do and they loved it! So we got the deal. Thank you. They want you to write the script. So I want you to send me more samples of your work so I can get it to them." And I said, "okay," and that all came from me being ready to write, because you never know how it will come to you. You can be in a meeting with someone and they can say, "Man I have this idea about vampire cheerleaders," and boom I'll go back and write it and get it back to them. Even if the writing wasn't that great, they leave thinking, "Man this guy is hungry. This guy wants to write. This guy can write."

SM: I always look for out of the box ways of getting heard and getting seen, and in essence pitching. Because that is what you were doing. You were selling something to a buyer. Taking snippets of your script for people to read was definitely a unique way and will help anyone reading this book.

EH: In this business, you will have a lot of agents that will tell you to find your niche and write what you're good at, because if you are good at Comedy or Horror, then you will be that go-to guy when people are seeking a Comedy. I encourage writers to write all different genres. That's very rare in this business. They are out there but compared to people who simply focus on their niche, there are few writers that can write across the board and be really effective in each genre. So I encourage writers to have different samples of different genres to show people that you aren't a writer who only focuses on one niche.

I can tell you Squeaky, I've done it all, and I've gotten far in the business with no agent or manager. Of course, now I need that with what I have going on, but I've gotten far without an agent and manager, but with relationships and pitching; polishing my idea and knowing it backwards and forward, and being able to pitch more than one idea in a short amount of time.

SM: So how do you do that? Let's say you land in the room with someone who can take your ideas to the next level. How do you pitch several ideas in a small amount of time? Also, how do you start your pitch?

EH: What I learned to do was polishing an idea. I would take 3 ideas and plan it out real carefully; try to figure out the important points of the idea. I would make sure that my pitch would have a very captivating storyline. I would take a sentence, let's say a 2-line logline, and I would figure out how I could say it in one line.

SM: To make it more succinct.

EH: I would do that to all of my ideas. When you pitch, it is not about just pitching the words and saying what the idea is. You have to be really captivating when you pitch it. I realized in my pitch that whenever I would pitch, they would see the idea because of the way I pitched it. I would emotionally get into it, and they would be like, "Wow, you are really into this story and you got me into this story!"

SM: So you would go in and tell the stories of these ideas? Let's take your film, *Steps*, how would you sell *Steps*?

EH: Whenever I would get into rooms with people I would pitch it by saying, "Hey, I got this great story about forgiveness, recovery, redemption and love and the steps people take to get to it." I had to say something that would capture people's attention quickly. When you say those words, people immediately think, "Oh, I can relate to one of those words or I can relate to all of them." You've already piqued their interest. Then they'd say, "Recovery, redemption and love? What is it about?" "Oh, it's about this guy who gets shot..." I can't remember my pitch off hand because it's been so long, but I would go into the story. "It's about a guy who gets shot and loses everything and 14 years later he ends up having to take care of the guy who shot him and ruined his life." I would say it so quickly and they would be like, "That was kind of interesting."

I've been on the phone with Tim Story and after pitching to Tim Story he told me, "That's the best pitch I've ever heard," while he was shooting *Fantastic Four*. I pitched an idea to Ben Affleck, and he said, "I love it. I would do it but my brother Casey has to direct it." It was about a Wall Street guy who gets caught up in an embezzling scheme, and has to serve two years in jail, and he pays a homeless man to go serve time for him. But it was the way I pitched the story that they connected with me because of my emotion; the way I pitched it.

SM: Your passion?

EH: Right! It sucks them in every time. Once you hook em' then hit them with the rest of your story.

SM: What I'm hearing is the first things you pitch are the universal themes. You said, "*Steps* is a story about forgiveness, recovery, redemption and love...and then you pitch the arc, climax, conflict? Right? "A man must forgive the person who actually made his life

144

	horrible by taking care of him"…or something like that. Right?
EH:	Right.
SM:	I say all the time that you always want to get in the room because what paper and pitch materials can't do is sell a project like your passion can. I like to say start with the premise and then pitch midway through, and you have just demonstrated that for me. I would like to ask how you prepare for your pitches.
EH:	For me it's all about repeating it, writing it down and reading it word for word how you are going to pitch it. Close your eyes and recite it and consistently pitch the idea over and over in my head. What will happen is, as you start to finesse it and get better, and know it completely, you know you won't end up looking bad. Then prepare yourself to be able to answer the suits in the room for when they see a loophole or a weakness in your concept.
SM:	Do you feel like when you are in the room, the people go for the weakness?
EH:	Yes! Yes, sometimes they do. But if they don't know the whole story…the thing to do is get them so caught up, so hooked on your idea that they don't ask any questions about your loopholes, they want to read the script. What you do is, when polishing your ideas, it's always good to somehow drop in comparisons of successful films. Never compare your idea to another TV show or film that didn't do well. For instance, one of my ideas is a male version of *Sex and the City*. So, I might say, "If you like *Hung*, if you like *Californication*, if you like, *Entourage*, this is the unorthodox male version of *Sex and the City*." Right away they are thinking, "You named 3 or 4 different shows that were good, and you have something that is similar to that?" These agents, these suits, they don't want to hear an idea…
SM:	That is untested or original?
EH:	The worst thing you can do when you pitch an idea is telling them it's the first draft. They aren't interested in reading the first draft; they are interested in reading the best draft because at the end of the day they are there to make money. So they have to know you are giving them your best. They don't want to wait around for you to do

the 5th or 6th draft. They want to know that you gave them the best that you got. They want to be able to go, "I can run with this and make money off of this." So back to your point, you want to polish your idea so that you are speaking confidently and you don't stutter. You want to know what you are talking about. You can include real life situations, statistics from current shows, ratings, but you have to do it very quickly. And that should all come after you have pitched the story and have them hooked. I have a movie script that I pitched and was able to get Kendall and Kylie Jenner attached to it. I pitched, "It is a horror story set in one location; a tattoo parlor. After partying, a group of students want to go get tattoos. Unbeknownst to them it is owned and operated by a cult that believes that body art is a sin. This show would be great if you like, *Hostel*, like *Saw*, this is a franchise piece." All those key words; "Franchise?" "Saw?" "Hostel?" "Horror?" [They're are thinking] "Wait a minute, that sounds interesting!" So you have to know those key words to drop to get them to go, "Wow!" You will see that most times, their eyes will light up. They already know the statistics on Horror films and the money they bring in. They already know the financial possibilities of franchise ideas. So you have to throw in something that makes them say, "That sounds like it's going to make a lot of money, let me read that." That's what gets them. So once you master that and drop in those little key words to get their ears perked then you are good; you are getting good at it [pitching].

SM: When you first hooked your rapper, how did you do it?
EH: Well, they had a story that they wanted written and I gave them samples of my work and they were like, "Yeah this guy can write." And that's how it happened. And it's still happening to this day. I'm currently doing a film with an award-winning producer and what happened was, my film through relationships got to their attorney. The attorney sent it to the producer and when he watched it he said, "Whoever wrote this film could write my movie." So it's the same thing that happened with the rappers, they had an idea, I had about 5 different snippets from different scripts; urban, action, sci-fi, comedy. Each snippet was no more than 2-3 pages. Those samples is

what got people to say, "Wow!". Giving someone a 90-page script is too much. Give them a little sample and they go, "Wow. This guy can write" and it may even make them say, "Send me a script." So you want to give them very little but make it enough to hook them. I used to tell people, "Just get me the meeting, get me in the room with the right person, and all you have to do is sit back, put your hands behind your head, put your legs up and let me do what I do" Every time they do that, they say, "Eddie, you said it!" I know what to say and what to do and I know I won't waste people's time. Now if I'm in the meeting longer than a half hour, then I got you. I can really start to hit you more stuff. I've had people tell me, "Who's your attorney, we want to option all of your stuff this week?" And I'm like, "Naw, we aren't going to do that," but it's because I've learned how to polish my ideas. I've learned how to make a captivating pitch with passion. That's it. That's all you need. You need to walk in there and pitch that thing like it's a part of your blood. And last, I never want them to know how it ends.

SM: Now, that's an interesting tip!

EH: I want to hook them enough to make them say, "I want to read the script to see what happens." That's it. I never tell them the end. Leave them hanging on the edge of their seats. The same goes for when you send them a sample. Send them enough to make them want to read the entire script. The pitch is just to get them hooked.

SM: What part of the script do you send as a sample?

EH: I go through the script and send them a part that I know they will be impressed with. I end the sample with enough to make them feel like they should read the script. I have samples of my work that I send to people, and every time, they say, "I want to read the rest of this script after I got to the last page." This way when you hit them with the script, you know they are going to read it.

SM: Are there any mistakes you've made over your journey?

EH: Yes. My pitches were too long. I was trying to explain the whole story instead of just pitching the idea and getting them interested and wanting to learn more about the story. Any time you find yourself explaining the story, then you've messed up. The purpose of the pitch is to get them to want to know more about the story.

147

Ryan Richmond
Director of Production at Aspire TV, Content Creator

Ryan Richmond is known for his work on *Money Matters* (2011), *Lyfe's Journey* (2014) and *Money Matters* (2001).

SM: What separates a good pitch from a great pitch?

RR: Unfortunately, I think it's luck. But that can be translated into timing. You know what I'm saying?

SM: Yeah.

RR: If that makes sense. You can have two same exact pitches and on Monday you're good, on Friday it's great even to the same network. Do you know what I mean?

It's unfortunate but being on this side of the fence and seeing just how finicky the day goes as far as opinions on certain things, it's **JUST** interesting. And the only way to really be prepared in making the best, is making the pitch solid, to be able to control what you can.

To make a good pitch is knowing who you're pitching it to, knowing whatever their brand is, knowing whatever that flavor is. And then, knowing or having an idea of not what they're doing now, but where they'll evolve to in the next six months or a year from now.

Often, I get replications of what's already on the air. Well, that's on the air. You know what I'm saying? I don't need a variation of that. We want something that's not that.

Despite the fact that TV in general does a lot of replicating shows. They're like copycat and I get that. But I think the copycat come from seasoned producers, the network is generating that. If one network, say *Empire* hits and that's on Fox.

And CBS is like, "We want *our Empire.*" And so, they're going to come up with something. They're going to go to their seasoned producer that they already worked or have a background with and they're going to get them to do their version. It's not going to

149

be the up-and-coming producer that's going to do that. They are not going to trust it with that person.

Timing is probably the difference, but also the element that you can't control is the projection. It's knowing what they are known for and saying, "This is where you want to be. I think this is going to hit half a year or a year from now; this is going to be hot based on what you do and what's hot right now," or something like that.

SM: That makes a lot of sense.

As a content creator, what are some of the out-of-the-box things that you've done that have brought you big wins?

RR: That's a good question. I think taking a leap to create your own is always quite arguably a defining route of what you want in your career. You want to be known as a director or producer for a certain type of thing or just create. You have to pony up and do it yourself.

SM: Yeah.

RR: Now, there are so many things that go with that. There are so many levels as far as the quality, as far as the end result of what you put together. Say for instance, if you want to be an action director, how would you put together an action movie on your own without the budget and resources? You have to be able to gauge the best quality for the resources that you have.

And for me, doing my first feature on my own was the best choice I could have made. I put a lot of things on hold to make that film. It was – it wasn't a hit. It didn't win Sundance or anything like that but for what it was, I'm very proud of it.

I have something that is me that I am proud to showcase. I feel like I have this job because I did that film.

Successful in my eyes means it was distributed. It pops on Encore every once in a while, Starz. It was on Netflix for a little bit. But it's not much to it.

I put my two nickels together and made it but it's a product that I made no excuses about. It's a very small film and it feels and it looks that way but it's my voice. And so I think I will always tell folks, if you want to be in this lane of creating, you got to create something

	you can't wait and continue to ask. I think that it's much easier to do that now. I think people get that. That's why you have so many filmmakers out there doing their creating.
SM:	Web series and digital.
RR:	Yeah. You have your platform and you put it up. None of that was around when I did my film. It wasn't meant for that platform anyway so I wouldn't have probably put it online. In any case, I think that's probably the major one I think that has guided my career in many ways. It set me apart.
SM:	Kudos to you for not discrediting it. There's a tendency to not take pride in our work because it doesn't look like what we may see in hit box office films or whatever, but no, that's a huge deal! One that millions of content creators won't do. Kudos that it lives, is seen in homes, and that you have a film that was distributed. People who have created films and features still don't know how to tap into distribution. You know what I'm saying?
RR:	Correct, yeah.
SM:	That's a major feat. I have worked with top executives at Viacom, who have little backgrounds in film and have a history degree. But you're in development because you have the instinct and creative ability to develop and see a project through to fruition. I once was looking to go into development. I had asked for an informational interview with the general manager of Nickelodeon, Keith Dawkins – I don't know if you know him. But I met with him to talk about what I wanted to do because I was uncertain what direction I wanted to take, but had an interest in development. He said to me, "Squeaky, I'm going to be honest, I'm an executive producer and I don't know what you do nor do I do any of the things you do as a content creator. You should decide if you want to do your own Tyler Perry thing or if you want to get caught in the matrix of corporate." He was the catalyst for me

deciding to take the entrepreneurial route that I've taken to start my own production company.

You're at Aspire TV in development because you have a development and creative instinct. You can't really teach it.

It really comes down to instinct. Obviously, you have it. Your instinct, I'm sure probably comes from the natural instinct to create and to have an idea of what's good and what doesn't work.

RR: Yeah.

SM: Speaking of distribution, could you give the reader any tips on the best ways to get on the platforms you were able to get on to?

RR: Distribution is a mystery. I have known a little more about distribution because I've gone down the path, but I think ultimately, the distribution companies own those pipelines in a mass way.

To my knowledge, Netflix doesn't pick up individual films that often. They'll go to a distributer that has packages. They take 10, 20 films for an amount versus, you know – which obviously makes it easier. It makes it easier for Wal-Mart, for Target. That's how they do it. They do it in bulk. They're not coming to the individual filmmaker to take their film. If that happens at Netflix, it's very rare I think.

For me, after I did the film, I did the festivals. But I went to festivals not even with my film in the festivals, so I could reach distributors. By hook or crook, through connects, through degrees, talking to different producers, one would say, "I know this guy over at E1 or One Village (One Village is no longer around, Bob Johnson picked them up).

But I would say, "I know X amount of distributors who are attending this film festival. Let me see who I know that know those distributors." My film wasn't even in the festival. I specifically went to ABFF just to meet people. I submitted, but did not get in, so I went to meet people. I literally went to go hangout with the distributor by the pool. I made the relationship, and that's what this business is all about. I made the relationships by hanging out at the pool.

And then in the next festival that my film was in, that rep came and remembered me and said, "Yeah, I'm going to go check out your film." A year later they distributed the film.

Distribution I think ultimately still has – right now, you have more ways to get it out there. But if you want to do a mass scale, you got to go to the big houses, the big companies. It's smarter to have those conversations with them before you shoot then after. I didn't have those conversations before I shot. I don't know how much it would have made a difference, but they have formulas that they work with. If you know your priorities, you have a better chance of making those goals if you have those conversations with the distributor prior to putting your film out.

That's ultimately what it is. The big boys don't really like to deal with the individuals.

SM: There are probably millions of content creators who will benefit from hearing that information that you just shared. That's really valuable.

It speaks to thinking out-of-the-box. That's a nugget, a $100,000 answer, really. What are the top ways that people come to ASPIRE TV to pitch? And what would you say is the best way to prepare for a pitch with your network?

RR: How to come into the room?

SM: Yeah.

RR: It's a little different for each network. However, I would say we're branching into the reality development now. The best way for reality to be pitched here is to have some level of a sizzle.

SM: Okay.

RR: In reality, it's usually based on character or characters. If you got to pitch me a grandma that everybody loves, that's loved by the neighborhood. This woman bakes the best pie. She's so funny. Everybody loves her. I need to see that. I need you to give me three minutes on this person that you're pitching.

In reality, I think sizzles works best. It doesn't have to be that long. You just need to introduce your characters really. The more you have is cool, but it's

	really about if you're pitching me a person that exists, I need to see the person.
SM:	What about Skype interviews? Would that work or would you prefer to see it in sizzle format?
RR:	The Skype interview, that's an interesting choice. The easiest thing about the sizzle is with networks, it's several people that you need to lay eyes on the project. If you come to me and we have a Skype interview and I'm like, "I fell in love with it." Now, I have to go to Melissa [the head of development at ASPIRE TV]. You know?
SM:	No, what I'm saying is, what if I record an interview with the talent.
RR:	Yeah, I think that helps. Just keep in mind, you want them to look a certain way. You know what I mean? Everything is judged.

I say that because, it's one thing if you are a seasoned producer with credits, A, B and C on A&E or History Channel. I know the level and quality of your work. But if I can't refer to that and say to my boss, "Well, she put together a Skype interview of this characters so she could get it to us fast." I don't know…

If I have that body of work I would be like, "Well, she knows what she is doing. She has these credits. You got to check her out. She did these Skype interviews because she wanted to get it to us fast and they're hot off the press." If you don't have that, it's tough for me to sell it.

The development person has to sell it to the network. The point is you got to arm them, whoever your contact is, you got to arm them with as much as possible. They're doing exactly what you did, within the network to whoever has to lay eyes on it. Even if they're the boss and say they're going to do it, somebody else is going to weigh in with an opinion.

So I caution that. It doesn't have to be an Emmy-winning sizzle, but make it look like it was done professionally.

| SM: | Can you share from your experience some "don'ts" in pitching? I've got a lot of dos but what are the don'ts for you? |

RR:	I would say specific to Aspire, we get a lot of "Oh, I know Magic. I know Mr. Johnson. He told me to call you all." Or, "You all need this..." For us, that is a "no" because we know that Mr. Johnson didn't send you over here.
	I think knowing those folks could be beneficial, but knowing when and how to put that in your pitch or relationship, whoever your contact is, can be done smartly and not done tactless.
	We get it a lot, where people feel we should bring them in because they know Mr. Johnson.
SM:	And you are probably like, "And he didn't think to give you a soft introduction."
RR:	Exactly. What they don't know is he's not involved in the day-to-day over here. So for me, I know you don't know him that well, and you certainly don't know what we're looking for or what we need because you would have come at us differently. For me, that is a little annoying. That's going to be a "no" for me.
	What else? Another thing is being educated on what the brand is. Don't go in not knowing what the network is about. Don't come in without watching the network.
	We get a lot of scripted pitches for shows, for dramas, for comedies. We don't have any scripted original content on the network. You're pitching me something that we don't do. Now, you wasted both of our time. Now, I know you don't watch the network.
SM:	But what if like you said, it's about timing. For instance...
RR:	I understand. But genre wise...You got to know the business. Again, there's a reason why it's non-scripted. The reason is cost. If you ask, then that's one thing. Asking me like...
SM:	"Are you guys doing scripted?"
RR:	Yeah, or, "How far out?" "I don't see anything on your network that is scripted, do you foresee original scripted content in the future?" That's how you start the conversation.
	Not, "Well, I got a great movie for you all," or "I got a great TV drama for you all." You already told me at

155

that point that you haven't really watched the network. You just know that it exists.

SM: I remember when we first talked and pitched to Tina Thompson and Paul Butler [Former, General Manager], a couple of years back. If I could be honest, my then-partner and I made that same mistake. We did eventually ask that question as well. "When are you guys looking to do scripted?" They said, "We see that about maybe two or three years out." That time has passed already and you still have not ventured into scripted. So our pitch was extremely premature.

Now, I simply ask, "What are you looking for?" That's a good point. I'm glad you talked about that.

RR: That's it. That's the tough part. It's hard to know because the network is often – well, bigger networks have much broader scopes, much more strict, I guess. It's not day-to-day. But as far as the flavor of things, those things change.

SM: What should people include in their pitch; how should they prepare? What's important for you to know in the pitch that you want covered while they're in the room?

RR: This is pretty much the same around the board. I want for people to have a solid one-sheet. It shouldn't be too in-depth but a solid one-sheet, which are the concept, the main characters and genre. So that's the one-sheet.

And then, it should be followed up with some level of what it would cost because that's the second question.

SM: That's top line, right? We don't need to go into the...

RR: No, it's all top line.

SM: Okay.

RR: It's best if you already kind of have dived in a little bit that way, if they like it, and they start to ask questions, you have those answers. Pitches need to be streamlined. They need to be consumed very quickly and easily.

SM: What do you mean by that?

RR: Like the one page. You don't do more than one page for the most part. If they want more, then that's good. That's a good sign. You can certainly have that prepared. Like, "Who do you see is this character?"

"Well, I see it as this so and so character," and pull that out, that type of deal.

I don't think you want a lot of questions as far as trying to understand the story. That means it wasn't explained well. If they're asking things to dig deeper into it, then that's a good thing.

If they don't understand it, then you're not doing a good job at explaining what it is. If I'm sitting here confused versus excited, then the person is not doing well. The person is not ready to be pitching.

SM: The pitcher has to understand the difference between the two. I couldn't imagine going through an entire pitch and thinking, "I got him" and it's really just because they don't get it.

RR: Yeah.

SM: I asked content creators once, "How do you know if your ideas are great concepts and how do you test it?" I believe content creators should test their ideas before going into a pitch meeting by rehearsing in front of a small audience.

Rehearsing is key. Rehearsing the pitch allows a person to hear and/or see what's unclear.

Ryan, that's all the questions I have, do you have something you'd like to add?

RR: You asked really good questions.

SM: Thank you.

Nathan Adloff

Writer and Director of *Miles the Movie*

Nathan made his feature film debut with *Nate & Margaret* (Co-Wrote/Produced/Directed). It sold for worldwide distribution prior to completion. It also received a commendatory review from Roger Ebert.

Nathan acted in Joe Swanberg's early films and IFC series, *Young American Bodies* and appeared in Frank V. Ross's *Audrey the Trainwreck*, in addition to making a handful of award-winning short films. He also co-created and directed a TV pilot, *Bad Sides*, which was a finalist in the Chicago Comedy TV Pilot Competition. His first leading role in the film *Blackmail Boys* won various film festival awards and sold for worldwide distribution. His short film *Cock N' Bull* was selected to screen in the 2013 Outfest Los Angeles LGBT Film Festival, which he also acted in. In 2014, his short *Grown This Way* won a best film award in Outfest's Fusion Lab.

In April of 2015, Nathan wrapped up directing his second feature film, *Miles*. The story centers on a high school senior who joins the girls' volleyball team in hopes of winning a college scholarship after his father's untimely death. It stars Molly Shannon, Paul Reiser, Missi Pyle, Tim Boardman, Annie Golden, Yeardley Smith and Stephen Root.

SM: When you started with *Miles* the movie, what was the pitching process like for you? Did you have to pitch it?

NA: Well, *Miles* was my second feature and Ash Christian had produced it. He'd produced my first feature. The way that happened was that I met him at the Sidewalk Film Festival in Birmingham, Alabama, for a film that I had acted in and he was on Jury. And we just hit it off. He had made 3 or 4 of his own films that he'd written and directed and he was looking at that time to produce someone else's work. So, I sent him a rough draft of the script that we had. He read it on the plane ride home and emailed once he had made it home and said that he wanted to help me make the film. And we were shooting in Chicago the next summer. So there really wasn't a lot of pitching or convincing done with him. He made everything fall in place and went to bat for me for investors, and cast and crew, and all the moving parts.

158

It was kind of the same thing with *Miles* because we had worked together before. So, I had asked him to read the script and we had a table read with him and some people with actors when he was in LA, and he gave me some notes and agreed to help me make *Miles*. So, I haven't been in an official pitch situation that maybe you have been in. I'm scared that I may one day have to do those.

SM: I'm so jealous of your story! You are a part of that "very few" that stuff like this happens to. But, I do know at the same time there is something to be learned from the story you are telling. I listen and think there must be something great about your writing. And you do tell very unique, authentic stories.

NA: Yeah, I think that is the core of it. You have to have a story and you have to find someone that believes in that story.

SM: Well, you've found someone who believes in two of your stories. He believes in your writing. I mean, I can pitch until I'm blue in the face, but if my writing sucks...

NA: At the end of the day, I think that's most important. For sure. Some people can come in with huge stars attached and money and the script so it might still go, but if you come in with nothing but a script, then it has to be good.

SM: Well, nine times out of ten, independent content creators are not coming to the table with major stars and millions of dollars secured. So, my lesson here is, to hell with the pitch for a while, get the story where it is so good so it can't be refused. And also, find the right person that really connects to the story.

NA: And things like events like conferences at film festivals or even online there are places you can post your pitch or script for feedback. These places and things were very valuable.

SM: How did you know your script was ready to share?

NA: With Ash, I was halfway through with my first draft. It was kind of a "read it and tell me what you think," kind of thing. I wasn't holding my breath as far as getting a "yes, let's do it." With *Miles*, my script was much further along when I shared it with Ash and did a table read. We made a lot of changes after that, but they were pretty minor. I think also it's really important to share rough

	drafts with peers you respect and value their opinion and will be honest with you not just tell you it's amazing. Giving you the real feedback you need to make it the best it can be before sharing it with investors and producers.
SM:	Had you known Ash's producer history before meeting him?
NA:	I saw the program book for the festival before being at the festival. I read his bio and looked him up and had a rough idea of who he was, but I didn't know him before meeting him there.
SM:	Were you intentional about meeting him at the festival?
NA:	Not really. We honestly just hit it off as friends. The festival is a lot of fun. It has a summer camp feeling and it gives you the feeling where you don't want to leave because you are having so much fun, bonded and made such great friends.
SM:	How did you attach talent to *Miles* and how did you find financing?
NA:	It was our casting director. Ash had worked with him on a project before shooting *Miles*. It was a Chinese action movie that was shot here in LA. It starred the Brad and Angelina of China, but shot here. His name is Rich Delia, he's amazing, he casted movies like, *Pitch Perfect,* and *August: Osage County.* He does like big films, but also does little films like this. So, he was a perfect match for a project like this where it was a passion project, and he really like the script, and people answer his calls. You know, Molly Shannon was my first choice, and I met with her three days later after talking to him about who I would love to meet with first; the same thing with Paul Reiser. Met with him very quickly. Really everyone who I was able to meet with here in LA all agreed to it after we had a meeting. We did a few days casting in New York, where I saw you. If we didn't have a casting director of that caliber, I don't think we would have gotten the names that we did.
SM:	Before you found the casting director, were you fully financed?
NA:	No! (Laughter) We weren't fully financed until way after we started production. That's a whole other thing. That's another thing to talk about, (laughter), "When is it time to start pre-production." We didn't have half of our budget

before shooting. It was a day-by-day dilemma. But somehow we got through it and did it all. So no. We raised some funds initially, asking everybody for money. It was kind of around the time we were casting. Some of the people we were approaching we couldn't even lock them in. We were just bringing on the essential people at first and handling the business.

SM: I think your story will really help the filmmaker on the step-by-step process. It's always a catch-22. In order to get the first monies, you need the actor. But in order to get the actor, you need the first monies.

NA: Oh, it's totally a chicken or the egg situation. At some point you just have to bet on one and then go for the other.

SM: In your case you went for the actor.

NA: Yeah, it was a safer route, just because if you have some names attached, that's more appealing for the investors. People can love the script and love the story, but if there are names attached, it helps so much more to get people to say "yes" and give up the money.

SM: What was it like for you to bring in investors? Did you play a role or was it all Ash?

NA: We all played a role in bringing people to the table. With me it was another random meeting where I met an investor on a cruise ship. (Laughter) I was on the ship because there was a film festival that one of my shorts got into. On the boat, I met him and I told him I was writing a new movie. I was able to show him my first feature on the boat and he said he wanted to help me with *Miles*. Through the other producers, we sort of pieced together the money that we needed from more than a handful of investors. You know when you make such a small movie, you have to be creative; it's hard to say no to small investments. You know someone is asking to be an executive producer and they are only offering a thousand dollars, or a couple of thousand dollars, it's still hard to say no. You know normally you would offer them an associate producer or whatever title is appropriate for the amount. Sometimes we got, "Can I be in the movie if I invest a few thousand?" Things like that can happen as well – get investors who are also actors. Which is interesting and was something I had never heard of

| | before my first feature. So it's really just being creative and pulling together people who are connected and have some money. Really on my first feature I really didn't know people with money. I didn't grow up with money, or hang around people with money. So it's really just through networking and my producers how we pulled it in. And it was still hard to get money. |

SM: Did you have a budget that was already set?

NA: Yeah. But we ended up on the very low end of what we could make the movie for. But you do what you have to do to get a movie in the can.

SM: I know that story.

NA: And I think it's good to aim for. So, if you don't quite get there you can still make it. You can do things creative like condense scenes or cut scenes, use the same locations for more scenes that were intended to be in two different locations. You have to get creative and figure out a way to make it work. It's good to have people with you that have that mindset.

SM: Who are used to solving problems...yeah. Did you also have to pitch to get distribution deals?

NA: No, we don't have a distributor yet. We are just starting to be seen by film festivals to be considered playing. So through those we hope to have it seen by distributors and to get it in front of their eyes. We do have a sales agent, which we did have sort of a little bit before we shot. But they are also getting it in front of distributors eyes at the same time that we are sending it to film festivals. So we are hitting hard now and in a little bit of a waiting to game to see what come of it.

SM: How did you secure a sales agent?

NA: That was through Lisa Black. She had met him at a film festival and they connected. It was the first project of hers that they picked up. They may have represented another film she'd produced. But, it's kind of the same thing – "Uh, who knows a sales agent?" And you know, just kind of getting a consensus of who knows who, and if there are any fees involved, and what's realistic.

SM: What's the job of the sales agent? Do they tell you what they are willing to do? Or do you decide which one you want to go to?

NA: With such a small movie it's hard to be picky. And we

162

	have to be realistic with who we think would take the movie on. So, my producer said they were great and the sales agent invested in the film too, so it was hard to say no to that. And they are great; they are working really hard to get *Miles* into festivals all over the world right now.
SM:	Oh that's great.
NA:	Their job is really pushing it to film festivals to try to get it programmed. It helps a little bit with the film having representation going into film festivals submission. It sort of gives the film credibility having a company backing it, rather than doing individual. It's kind of like having an agent for your movie. And also getting in front of distributor's eyes and getting offers. If we get an offer that we are interested in, they will handle the deal with the distributor. So it's nice to have someone kind of take that load off.
SM:	I feel like you've taught me so much! I feel like I learn more from people who are independently doing this because we wear so many different hats and we have to be in every room. It's not a department for us; we have something to do in every department. So we grow knowledgeable all around. What you have offered here today is so helpful!
NA:	Yeah, I think so. I think we all have to just fake it till you make it. I mean what business do I have telling Molly Shannon or Paul Reiser what to do? It was very surreal working with people like them being a second-time filmmaker, not actively getting jobs in the business but doing just my films. It's surreal, but I don't take it for granted and I'm doing the best I can in these situations.
SM:	Did you ever ask them why they said, "yes" to your film?
NA:	I never asked, but we did like a press kit interviews with some of the cast and that was the question and they all said it was the story and the script. Also me as well. Just meaning that it was based on my life, so they all felt like I would know how to answer questions on set and the backstory and the motivation of characters because it's loosely based on the characters from my high school.
SM:	Wow. This was so good. I'm out of questions.

Douglas Holloway

Former President of Multi Channel Distribution at ION, NBC Network Distribution Partnerships and Affiliate Marketing

Mr. Holloway helps senior executive positions in Network and Cable TV with additional positions in publishing and consumer goods. Some highlights include:

• Founding team member of the SyFy Channel and National Geographic Wild Networks
• Part of a team that developed and executed the initial fee for carriage model in the TV/video/content distribution business
• Created new ventures, grew existing businesses and led turnarounds to profit
• Developed prototype of an online financial management system for consumers

He served on the board of five public and private for-profit companies and eight not for profit organizations (chairperson of two). He raised millions of dollars as well as endowed an infinite scholarship fund at Emerson College.

SM: Why is it so hard to get into the door unless it's by referral or agent?

DH: Well, it's a small closed environment, it always has been. Over the last 30 years with more and more cable networks coming along, more and more people have more and more access. It's just a greater demand than when you had three networks.

        As those expansions have occurred, with respect to more networks with more programming demand, a lot of new players were able to slip in. But not a lot of minority players have been able to slip in.

        It's been just like when you're in front of the camera or behind the camera as opposed to in a business suite. It's just been very difficult to fit in because high risk– high reward, a lot of opportunity and folks tend to circle the wagon and keep it for themselves.

SM: Yeah.

164

DH: They keep those things they're comfortable with and those people that they're comfortable with. And also, one or two slip through the pipeline. Then, they get the opportunity and the looksee. And if they connect with some other folks then those folks may get pulled along. In the case of Oprah and Lee Daniels, as an example. But you know, how many of those happen? Not many.

SM: So, when people come up to you and ask you, "How do I get in the door? Who do I speak to?" What is your advice to them? For instance, if I ask, "Hey, is it possible that you can make a connection for me?" What do you say to those people?

DH: If I have a connection to make depending on that individual and depending on the quality of the work, maybe or yes. In many instances, I have probably more times than not, certainly far more times than not. It also depends on if that individual and I see eye-to-eye and seem to be on the same wavelength. Also finally, depends on if I have a connection to make, but you have to have a good product. But if not I would say, "Well, this is what you should do to get your product where it should be. If you do that, this is how you get them – what they pay," which is nothing, I'd give them what they should do with it based on my perspective. I wouldn't leave anybody empty-handed. Whenever somebody came to me, I would not leave him or her empty-handed.

SM: From your perspective as the pitcher, what would you say worked for you? And what were some of the mistakes that you made along the way, if any?

DH: I think it's more about being at the right place at the right time with the right product. Because I've had good products but it wasn't the right place and the right time, some real good products.

       Case in point, a friend of mine developed a show years ago, 20 years ago and it was when the lipstick cameras first came out where you could put a small camera in a helmet, for instance. It was a reality show. It's called LAFD and they had so much incredible footage, going through all these approvals with the LAFP. It was just an amazing show.

	High and quality people, big stars were cast to it as exec producers. It got a pilot, a financed pilot by a network. After the pilot was made, a new hit of programming came in and killed the product. Then they were never able to get it or sold to anybody else. To this date, I still think it's one of the most engaging shows because if you think about Chicago FD, it's that show but on a reality basis.
SM:	Wow, yeah.
DH:	Now…
SM:	It's almost like watching Cops, then.
DH:	Yeah, but you're in cars.
SM:	Yeah. I mean, now with GoPros, you never know. It can probably still work.
DH:	Yeah, but you know, this was the beginning – the original was called lipstick cameras. But the one difference between those cameras and the cameras now was those cameras were hardwired to you – so you have much more flexibility today than 15-20 years. They shopped the show so many times, but it never got picked up.
SM:	What should I include in my pitch?
DH:	You want to talk about demographics. You want to talk about target market; you want to talk about where is the angle, where is the hook, what makes it stand out?
SM:	Is it necessary for me to come with a fully packaged show before pitching?
DH:	You're better off if you do. If not, it's going to be more of an uphill fight or battle.
SM:	Is it myth or truth: When you package your show with named talent, you have more control of the show? Is that myth or true?
DH:	Generally, it's hard to maintain control without any money on the table. There's like different criteria you need and depending upon what you don't bring to the table, the less and less control you have. So you have money on the table, you have talent attached. You have a good executive producer, good director, and good writer. You got a plan to save money, tax credits and location shooting, and then all

166

of those things are going to give you more and more control.

That's how it works. It's a balancing act. The more things you have on one side of the equation, the more it shifts in your favor. The less things you have on your side of the equation, the more it's in the other's favor.

SM: What would you say is the best way for packaging? Should I go to a packaging agent? Or should I connect them myself, going to their agents?

DH: You know, it depends on the contacts you have; it depends on any number of things – what your access is. The one thing about this business, which you're asking, is there is no magic bullet. There's no one-size-fits-all .

SM: What would you suggest to go in the room with?

DH: Go in with much of a bible as possible. I'd go in there with foresight into more than one season. I'd go in there with stars attached and try to go in there with some money or some commitment that somebody's going to give me some money.

SM: Okay. How would content creators go about getting distribution deals before their project is finished – when does that happen? How does that happen?

DH: You would just call it a pre-sell. After you get a network that's going to take it, you can go to other distributors and do a pre-sell at the backend.

SM: Okay.

SM: Is there anything else that you want to share?

DH: Not off the top of my head but I'll think about it. If I come up with something, I'll let you know.

SM: Okay. Well, thanks so much. I appreciate your time.

Tracey Baker Simmons

Creator and Executive Producer of *Being Bobby Brown*, *The Houston's* and *Bobby Christina*, also Former Director of Development at Jarrett Creative

Tracey Baker-Simmons is accredited with being one of the pioneers of celebrity reality, opening doors for African American talent and television producers in the reality television medium.

Tracey is a 20-year production veteran in film and television. Her journey into the entertainment industry began at Warner Brothers Music in the marketing and promotions department, which eventually spurred her interest in film production. Baker-Simmons produced national commercials and hundreds of Music Videos for LeRoux Pictures and Westside Stories in Atlanta, Georgia. In 2002 she produced the independent feature film *The Book of Love*, starring Sallie Richardson, Robin Givens, Treach of *Naughty by Nature* and Richard T. Jones of *Judging Amy*. In 2005, Tracey created the pop culture phenomenon-Bravo reality series *Being Bobby Brown*, starring controversial music legends Bobby Brown and Whitney Houston. Then in 2010, in a joint partnership with Rainforest Films, Baker-Simmons and her partner Wanda Shelley executive produced MTV2's *Sprite Step-Off*, which debuted to record breaking ratings for the network. In the same year, Baker-Simmons received an Emmy(TM) nomination from Southeast Region - National Academy of Arts and Sciences for *Platinum House*, a show that she created and executive produced with R&B legend Keith Sweat. Tracey also taught production for four years as part of the senior seminar at Emory University's Goizueta Business School.

Tracey recently served as the Head of Development for the New York based production company, Jarrett Creative and oversaw development of all non-scripted projects. While at Jarrett she was responsible for the development of series such as TNT's *Boston's Finest*, TLC's *Alaskan Women Looking for Love*, LMN's *I Killed My BFF*, TVGN's *Rock the Boat* (featuring New Kids on the Block), and several other series. She also brought Jarrett Lifetime's series *The Houston's: On Our Own* which premiered October 24, 2012 starring the family of late Whitney Houston. Tracey served with Seth Jarrett, Julie Insogna-Jarrett and Wanda Shelley as executive producers and showrunner.

SM: Can you talk about the packaging process? You have
             several shows you are currently in production for or
             are prepping to pitch. What has been your process to
             package the shows?
TBS: If we're specifically talking about reality television –
             even in scripted television, you have an idea but you
             need talent. That's what will differentiate you from the
             rest looking to pitch. Unless you are making a format,
             right? Even in a format think about it, *American Idol*
             worked because Simon was a part of the package. So, I
             think the key is any idea that you have, if you want to
             be big, bad producer, then the number one thing is to
             deliver talent. You know? Deliver something that's
             tangible. And guess what, talent is the thing that
             makes you have an idea that people can't steal. Cause,
             if I'm pitching a show and I'm like, "Okay, it's about
             whatever," and Denzel is the talent. If Denzel and me
             are connected at the hip, then no one's taking the idea
             because they can't get Denzel without me. That's what
             Mark Burnett did with Donald Trump, with *Apprentice.*
             Because Mark Burnett wasn't big, bad Mark Burnett.
             He was a producer, but he got Donald Trump to do
             that show and Trump in exchange showed loyalty
             because I think the network originally wanted to get
             rid of Burnett, and Donald Trump was like, "I'm not
             going to do it without him." Basically, that's how he
             got the show, *The Apprentice.* And that's probably
             why in DC, Mark Burnett probably didn't release
             those tapes because Mark Burnett was like, "In a time
             when Donald Trump could have easily said, 'Ok Mark,
             you're too small the network doesn't want you.'" he
             didn't do that, he stayed loyal to him.
SM: Do you have a certain script that you say to talent?
             How do you lock them in?
TBS: To be honest, it's easier now because people know
             who I am. They can Google me, or whatever. But, let's
             go back to Bobby [Brown] and Whitney [Houston],
             who I didn't know at all. The key was selling them on
             the idea, and in that case, it was a show about opening
             up people's eyes to who Bobby was. He was down for
             it, and basically she came on board. But the key was
             the idea. It's like, "This is x," you know, whatever

169

your idea is, and having the talent believe that you are the person that they can trust – trust is major with talent, "Can I trust you?" Look, plenty of producers they trade people's trust in – that's probably why I don't have 100 shows on air or mega franchises, is because I really do protect my talent. I like to stand by my word, so whatever I tell them the show is going to be, I really fight for it to be that show and be in that lane. That sometimes doesn't set well with the network because they want to make it as juicy as they can and sometimes that hurts relationships. I am very loyal to my talent, first, because I want to be known as a trusted producer and deliver on that. So Trump trusted Mark Burnett, so ten years later, probably even with conflicting morals Mark Burnett has to stand by that trust.

Even with us, with Whitney she had to trust me. I had hundreds of hours of footage on her, and we were offered plenty of times to show something that may not have been flattering to her, but we stood and stand on that she could trust us, and she did, and we delivered on that trust. That's a big deal and it's important.

So in a sense, you are always pitching. You are pitching your talent. Then you put it together, and you pitch more. So from the moment you have an idea, you will continue to pitch until it lands on the screen, to be honest.

I mean we are doing this movie [Bobby Christina movie] and we had to pitch the casting person, to get her to say, "Okay, I want to do it," because she was nervous. Now we are pitching the director to come aboard. So it's not just a pitch to the network, it's lots of pitching. Pitching is a way of producing. It's the complementary piece of the producer. What you don't want to be is a used car salesman, which is a [bleeping] liar. You want to be a person who sticks to your word, and just are honest, telling people, "This is what it is, and this is what we are looking for." If it's drama, tell them that too, and let them decide. You'll be surprised what people will be willing to do to be on

	television. But you can sleep, because you're telling the truth.
SM:	In my interview with Austyn Biggers at BET [Now at LOGO TV Network], he said that when people are coming to pitch Reality TV, he always likes to go straight for the jugular with the talent when producers bring them into the room because he wants to know how honest producers have been with them. A lot of the times, the talent will look like, "Oh, I didn't plan to be talking about that or doing this on the show." But then there is no show for him. If the talent isn't ready to do this or that, then there is no show because that's what you promised me. Which means we are going into it lying and bs'ing the talent.
TBS:	You know what I always ask my talent? I'll ask, "How far are you willing to go, and what's off limits?" I need to know that because I need to tell the network that, and I need to understand if we even have a show or not.
SM:	So you are currently working with Big Fish Entertainment. When you go to production companies and pitch your show, what's the next thing? For instance, I recently pitched a production that expressed interest in two ideas of mine. When I reached back out to them, I asked for the status to see if they were interested in optioning my project, and they still hadn't really looked further into it. How do you move things along at a faster pace? How did you do it with Big Fish?
TBS:	Honestly, it hasn't been a fast pace with Big Fish. The reality of it is, those people have their own shows that they are filming, or something that is mega in their wheelhouse that is taking up time. I don't want to give an illusion that there is a way to make something move fast. Now if you walk up in there with Donald Trump...
SM:	Donald Trump or Ryan Seacrest
TBS:	Yeah, then everything will move along a lot faster. Or even [Barack] Obama, his transition story, or something, things are going to move fast depending on how strong your idea is or how fast they can make a sell because that's what this is about. It's hard. And to

be honest, that's why I'm careful. Like I haven't taken on a lot of projects of other people that I can't really sink my teeth into because I'm being very honest that most of my stuff is going to come first. I'm actually doing an animated adaptation of this children's book about Obama. That's on the top of my list right now. So between that and executive producing a made-for-television movie, launching my company, and re-releasing my biggest show, I might not be the person you want to pitch your idea. I sent out a few emails to a group of people telling them that I am not focusing on other people's projects until after February. If they wanted to call me back then, great. Until then I just wanted to be honest because I have so much to conquer between now and January that I don't want to hold anyone up.

SM: So, you pitched the *Bobby Christina* made-for-television movie to TV One and got the green light. What's the process thereafter?

TBS: If you pitch a production company and they like it, then you have to negotiate the terms. "What are the terms? You like this and then what? What does that mean? You want to take it somewhere and sell it? What do I need to do? What are my expectations?" You have to make it clear so you know where you are in the equation. "What percentage will you get? What input do you have? Are they pitching it with you or without you? Do they need you to be available at times?" All of those things, you know?

SM: That's good to know. What about a network, is it the same process?

TBS: With a network, they are going to tell you. "Okay we want developing, or we want you to partner with someone, depending on how new you are as a producer." They are going to tell you the next steps.

SM: Do you feel like you want to be in the room to pitch the idea? Or is it okay to go on without you and continue to pitch it?

TBS: It really depends on what it is. If I feel confident and the idea speaks for itself, that it's a great project for all the people and I feel comfortable, then I'm fine to let them do it. For me, if I'm playing half the part, I'm

172

happy not to be doing half the damn work. So, I sort of look at it like, "Great! Pitch it; sell it, what are the next steps?

Even if you are pitching a show that I've partnered with you on, which I don't do a lot of, but if I feel like I need to talk or say something, then I'm not partnering with anyone on that show. Or I'll partner on the back end – from a network perspective. Like me doing this movie [Bobby Christina], I initially was like, I should do it with the Jarretts [Jarrett Creative Group], but we seemed to have some creative differences, so I told the network that I didn't want to do it with them. And the network was like, "Okay, we still want the movie, will you still do it, and let us give you a partner. And I was like, "Great no problem."

SM: And then they looked for a partner for you?

TBS: Well they had one. The networks have partners. They have people they want people to work with. So, one approach could be, let them find me a partner, if you can make that thing happen.

SM: When you are pitching the idea, do you create a budget, or does the network give the amount they want to spend on making your project?

TBS: Yeah, the network usually works with you to do the budget. They may say, "We are thinking something in a certain range," and then you have to figure it out and go from there.

SM: I'm breaking it down, step-by-step, Tracy, because someone reading this book may not know what the process is like. Sometimes, I'll begin explaining things to content creators, and judging from the confused look on their faces, I realize they don't know what I'm talking about. That's when I realized, I've started somewhere in the middle of my knowledge and they are all the way down at the low end of that spectrum. So, I break it down like this to speak to the novice, so they can know what we are talking about and it's not missed on them. So, I'm slowing it down so I don't miss any steps.

This information is good to know, because many people don't know what the next steps are or how it plays out after being green lit. Which leads me to another question, "What negotiating power should one expect to have and does it depend on what they are bringing?"

TBS: I think it depends on what they are bringing to the table. If you are bringing a big piece of talent to the table, you're going to have a little more power than if you just bring an idea. So they would say, "Oh okay, so you are bringing this idea, and we're supposed to give you what for it?" And your resume, and all those things come into play. The more you bring to the table, the better you are going to eat, you know.

SM: In the deals you've been making lately, how much did you bring to the table? For instance, you have a project with Jamie Hector attached, did you only bring him to the table? Don't get me wrong; bringing him is a big deal. But, do you bring only 1 talent or are you locking in all talent for your projects?

TBS: That project has an ensemble cast, so basically, I brought them the cast. Earlier on in talks, we spoke about if the show should be an ensemble cast or led by 1 talent; either way, I was delivering the talent, whatever the talent was. Also, this show also requires a certain level of access to certain things, and I picked the talent based on their authority to give the access. So, I am bringing access and talent. And they were tough negotiators, and I probably could have gotten a bigger piece, but I really wanted to do the show and wanted to make the deal. But, you have to be realistic with your expectations, if you come to me and are like, "I have a good idea," and you don't really have talent attached, and I like the idea and feel I can add some pieces to it, and I am the person that will have to go out and sell it, and the person to go out and find the person that the network is looking for to deliver the show, then we aren't 50/50 partners and you need to get off of it. Some people have unrealistic expectations. Also, I want to say to you, I was talking to a person the other day. This person has had this project and she's been holding on to it and holding on to it. I want to say to her, "Wow, is this the only project you're ever going to have?" Like you have to decide, "Do I want to make a sell or do I want to be the master controller of my idea and that's all that matters?" A lot of times, that's the dilemma. And people get mad when you ask them for a piece of the pie and they think they need to be in control. You are not in control! The network is. Be honest with yourself. You have the investor, or distributor, or a network, or a studio for a film that you will have to take notes from. And you are going to have to shape it to fit their brand. So you are not going to be in control. You have to just be the conduit, so you don't want to take such a harsh position. If you have 10% or 20% of any of your ideas that are out there in the market place and you are making money, you are doing way better than you will be if you own 100% of your ideas and none of them are selling.

SM: I remember being like that years ago.

TBS: All of us are, because we feel like, "This is so precious to me." But we have to let it go, and trust that you are going to have more than one great idea. I mean, how many great projects does Mark Burnett have?

SM: The problem is when you have your first baby, you don't think that you can ever create that greatly again. But really you almost have to because that baby is rarely the one that will go anywhere. I don't know why I thought that way in the past either. Maybe it was fear of being left out. I remember my then writing partner and I thinking, "We can't attach those producers because what if they have the limelight because we are unknown.

TBS: I get it. But you have to trust God. You have to have confidence and release it and more will come.

SM: I'm so happy to have this chance to interview you because you've worked in development as well as a creative and your knowledge is two-fold. What mistakes have you made that you could save others from making? And also, what are the biggest mistakes you see others make?

TBS: The biggest mistake is to not prepare for success and not to know what's next. You should definitely have multiple projects. A lot of people are like, if this doesn't sell, maybe this would sell.

Also, in a pitch meeting if you aren't sure what the network is looking for, I suggest listen first. Ask, "What's happening? What are you guys up to? What are you looking for?"

Now, they have told you what they are looking for. Hopefully, you have something that is in that rise and you pitch that. If they say, "You know we are open, we are sort of reshaping, we are trying to figure out what we are trying to do differently," then you can start with what you are passionate about. If they like it, great, the conversation keeps going. But, if for some reason they are like, "Ehhh." It's a good idea to have a couple of things you are throwing out at them. And that's all preparation.

The other thing is what do you do if they buy your show? A lot of times with an independent producer, you are so engulfed in that show, you aren't thinking, "How do I capitalize off this moment? What's the next show am I selling? What else can I develop that may be complementary to this?"

SM: That's wisdom. Thank you so much for that. It makes me think of Shonda Rhimes and how many projects she must've had waiting in the wings.

TBS: You know we all hate the waiting room. We would all prefer to be on the field; we want to be out there playing. We want to be in the game. But in reality, we really should be preparing for that moment and you were so in the game that you never made time to develop more. So in the waiting room we want to be developing so that when we do get picked and we are engulfed, we are already set up for the next win.

I wish someone had told me that. To be very honest, I'm probably one of the prime examples of people who didn't know or have other options. If you think about it, *Being Bobby Brown* is probably 13-years-old, and a lot of people who started out the gate at the same time or after me, went on to build successful companies and sold them for a lot of money. We weren't able to flip that that way because we didn't know. We hadn't worked at a network. We were located in Atlanta. We weren't a part of the system. We didn't have the know-how to be like, "What's our next project. Let me be pitching my next project, or developing my next project while my team is pretty big." So we weren't ready. When the show ended is when we went into development mode. But it was kind of too late, because by the time we had something else ready and developed, a few months had gone by, and we tried to get back into the ring, and other people were already taking off.

SM: You know I'm now recognizing so many mistakes I've made. My biggest is not attaching people to my projects. I used to pitch just my ideas and realized over the course of my journey that I needed to start attaching talent to my projects. I have concluded that the reason I wasn't attaching talent was due to fear and a value issue; I was too afraid to reach out to talent because I didn't value myself and my ideas. I thought, "Why me? Why would they say yes, to me?" But that's another book. But, yes, I've probably made every mistake you mentioned. Let me ask you, what were the biggest mistakes you witness content creators making while in development at Jarrett?

TBS: I think the biggest mistakes anyone makes is not listening to the buyer. Don't be so caught up into wanting to talk about your ideas. You know, have a conversation with people; make a connection. Connectivity is everything. Ask the person what they are looking for. Don't think you have all the answers. They have a job for a reason, and they have a brand. Stop thinking they are desperately waiting for you and your idea. It's a brand. They have a look that they are trying to maintain. They have an audience that shows up every night for them and their content and they want to keep making them happy and continue to entertain them. So have a conversation to figure out how you can help them with their process. "How can I help them make their customer happy?" That should be your goal. Not, "I have this idea, I think your programming kind of sucks and you really need this." I always laugh when people pitch me something and say, "They really need this!" I'm like, "First of all, they don't give a shit about their need, and they're talking about their customer and their advertising needs." Half the time, you know how people are: "They need to do something like this because they are putting all of this terrible stuff out here." They don't care if the terrible stuff is getting ratings. They are not running around out here looking for stuff that is going to help change the world. They don't care. They are a brand. They are trying to make millions of dollars.

SM: [Laughter] I'm laughing because I'm sure I've said that before, at one point.

TBS: A lot of us have done that, if we are being realistic.

SM: I'm glad you brought that up. It's so good and I believe it will resonate with the people reading this book. Thank you so much! Priceless. Your advice is priceless.

Ronald Simmons

Executive Producer, Founder/CEO of Simons Says Entertainment

Ron Simons is the Founder and CEO of SimonSays Entertainment. Ron is a three-time Tony Award-winning producer and actor. He leads the SimonSays Entertainment strategic planning and development of theatre and film projects including the critically acclaimed films *Night Catches Us*, *Gun Hill Road*, *Blue Caprice* and *Mother of George* (all premiered at Sundance). His first documentary *25 to Life* premiered at the American Black Film Festival where it won Best Documentary. He also produced the Broadway productions of *A Gentleman's Guide to Love and Murder* (Tony Award for Best Musical), *Porgy & Bess* (Tony Award for Best Revival of a Musical), *Vanya and Sonia and Masha and Spike* (Tony Award for Best Play, Drama Desk, New Drama Critics and Outer Critics Circle Awards for Best Play, Drama League Award for Outstanding Production of a Broadway or Off-Broadway Play), *A Streetcar Named Desire* (AEA's Extraordinary Excellence in Diversity on Broadway Award). Off-Broadway projects include Bedlam's *St. Joan* and Bedlam's *Hamlet* Awards (Off Broadway Alliance Award – Best Revival (for Saint Joan). He also produced the Chicago production of *5 Lesbians Eating Quiche*, which received the FringeNYC Outstanding Production Award. Ron is also a member of The Broadway League Diversity Committee.

As an actor, Ron has appeared on stage, in film and television. He and fellow cast members won the London Stage Award for Acting Excellence for the play *Boy Steals Train* which he co-developed. He has performed in numerous regional theaters including Cincinnati Playhouse in the Park, Seattle Repertory Theatre, Utah Shakespeare Festival and the Classical Theatre of Harlem. Film and television credits include *Blue Caprice*, *Night Catches Us*, *27 Dresses*, *Mystery Team*, *Phoebe in Wonderland*, *Law & Order*, *Law & Order: Criminal Intent*, *As the World Turns* and *Nowhere Man*.

Ron's corporate experience includes positions as a Software Engineer at companies such as Hewlett-Packard and IBM and as a Marketing Executive at the Microsoft Corporation. Ron is a recipient of the Heritage Award from Columbia College's Black Alumni Council, 150 Distinguished Alumni Award from University of Washington, and is a Johnson & Johnson Leadership Award Fellow, IFP Cannes' Producer's

179

Network Fellow and a Sundance Producers' Summit Fellow. He holds a
BA from Columbia College, an MBA from Columbia Business School
and an MFA from the University of Washington's Professional Actor
Training Program.

SM: Ron, what kind of projects does your production
company seek?

RS: My mission is to change the world. A project that seek
to preserve culture as you, educate, illuminate, inspire
and/or tell stories of people who are not represented in
media, film, television. Those projects are high on my
list. The most important thing of any project is story. If
it's not a good story, then it's not worth my time
because there are a lot in Hollywood, not to say that
Hollywood don't put out good stories, but they put out
a lot of, you know, beyond the good stories, they put
out a lot of fluff, and candy, high pyrotechnics or
things of that nature, which I enjoy too. Mind you, I do
see some blockbuster video like everybody else.
But, essentially I look for projects that change the
world one film at a time. That and unrepresented
communities' stories is what my company is all about.

SM: You mentioned storytelling, which is really the focus
of this book. I've learned a lot about storytelling
through so many different people lately. How do you
decide from a pitch, "This is a go? This is something I
want to get behind?"
Is it the story? What is it that people have come in
with that made you say, "This is it?"

RS: Well, it's someone whose story is engaging,
compelling; that takes you on a journey. That leaves
you in a different place at the end than where you were
when it started. Those are the hallmarks of a good
story.

SM: For instance, when I came to pitch you; or when
anyone comes to pitch you, what's the selling point for
you? What separates me from them or anything in that
pitch? What separates the one that you decide to
choose or go with from others?

RS: A story that I haven't heard before.

SM: I like that. In fact, I've heard from different people and
different networks and production companies there are

no new stories. That there's only seven stories in the world and every now and then comes an eighth story. I'm assuming you're talking about the eight one.

RS: I actually feel that even all the stories I tell all have the same universal themes. It's my job to find a different lens to tell the story. My second film, *Gun Hill Road*, if you just look at it on the surface, you'd say, "Oh, this is some transgender film." That's the way it's shorthanded but it's not what it's about. It's a story about love and family, betrayal and redemption.
But the lens through which it is told is a Latino family in crisis over their transgender son. That's the lens that gets switched in. I could have explored those same themes of betrayal, of love and family through some Eskimo fisherman in the tundra somewhere. Do you know what I mean? It's the lens that makes it fresh and different. I don't think we're telling, at the end of the day, any new themes. The themes are just what they are. I think what's new and fresh is the lens through which we look at the story.

SM: If I was preparing to pitch you, how should I prepare for you? What are the things you find most important?

RS: I need a lot of things. I need to know what the genre is, what the time frame is. I need to know the budget. I need to know the cast, who is packaged to it, who's directing it. I need to know what the synopsis is; I need the storyline. I need to understand what the universal themes of the piece are exploring. I need to understand has it won any awards, the pedigree of the film. Who's already involved on the film or the project of the script – those are the top line things.

SM: I'm glad you said that. You will not consider a project then that hasn't been somewhat packaged.

RS: I will consider, it's just that it's much more unlikely that I will pursue it at the very beginning because I get dozens of submissions of people who have great products like, "Here's my great script. I think it's going to be amazing and I want you to do all the heavy lifting to get it from where it is now to the film. Which is to package it, come up with the look book, the budget, to find the director. I can only do one of those, maybe.

181

SM:	You know it was actually my pitch with you that opened me up to making sure I create a distribution strategy for my projects. It takes a lot of research. Is there any information that you can give regarding creating a distribution strategy?
RS:	It takes years of experience to know who the distributors are, what kind of films they distribute, and how that is different from domestic versus international. It's what I spend hours during my consulting services for young filmmakers doing. But it's not something you can do in 10 minutes. I can't even do it in 90 minutes. I always tell people, if you don't have the information you need, align yourself with somebody that does have information. You can partner with someone. You can get a budget, if you need to, hire a line producer to come up with a budget for you. If you don't know what a look book is, you have to hire a graphic artist to come in and help you put together your look book. It's not going to be very helpful to create a look book but there's nothing there because you don't have any packaging; no one to direct it, no one signed up to produce, no one to act in it, no one signed up to be involved in it.
	I can tell you, over the last five years, I've probably got two to three thousand submissions of people who are complete novices and have no idea. And the submissions I get, because all of us are novice at some point, are basically looking for someone to come in and guide them through the entire process. That's a huge no, no. That's like saying to someone "Hi, my name is Ron and I'd like for you to teach me, to get a Bachelor's degree. Here's your Bachelor's degree and go. Thank you."
SM:	That is funny.
RS:	[laughter] If that's my child, well you know, I might consider it. Like I said, I can only do so much for one project at a time. That's why I either encourage people to find partners or if you want me to be that person, I'm happy to do that but that comes at a fee because my focusing on your work means it's in-depth. It means it's going to take the time of three other projects that I'm getting nothing out of because I'm

	focusing on you right now. Do you know what I mean?
SM:	I get it. I totally get it. The end result would be – either to pay for it or to find a partner. Well, saying, "Just find a partner," doesn't necessarily help me. That doesn't necessarily lead me up the right path. Can you help me better understand what goes into "Finding a partner?"
RS:	You need to put yourself in a place where people are doing the thing that you're doing. Of all the film fests around the country, how many film fests have you gone to in the last year?
SM:	In the last year I went to maybe four.
RS:	Okay. That's the place where you need to be not only networking, maybe pitching, but you should be going to every cocktail party that you can get into, every premier, every social event, every symposium, seminar, talk back, that you can because that's where you meet the people. You meet people, it's where they get together to do the interview stuff – that film festival, that premier, or in classes.

There are classes that are taught at many universities on film producing. I don't know if you've taken any of those classes but I know people who take classes in production for producing for Broadway.

Alia Jones-Harvey is the one of the producers on *Eclipsed*. She took a class in City College, I'm not sure. I would say the exact – to the person that you're writing to has to be proactive and find out where filmmakers are spending their time. What are they reading?

Do you have a subscription to Filmmaker Magazine? If not, you should have been had that. That's where filmmakers are talking about what they're doing and where they are going, what their aspirations are, what their dreams, what kind of project they work on.

There's a bevy of information. You just have to go out there and search for all that information to build the education when you're not in a program, a certified Bachelor's or certified program. Do you know what I mean? That means you need to be on periodicals, you need to be on the website, you need to be on the |

Facebook posts. There are dozens of filmmakers, groups that get on Facebook that allow them to grow. It's easy to search them using Facebook.

Same thing with the Internet. It's not like when I was a kid. We had to go to the library. ou can find all this stuff on the Internet. You can find out about someone in addition to reading a book, in which there are many books about film producing. I personally read two or three when I started producing. I kind of go, "I wonder what producing is all about." I decided to educate myself by reading books. The more I read books, the more I met and heard about these people.

Then I knew some names and I was like, "Oh let me add them to the list to talk with them about their process or their career or their connections." The more people you meet, you can build a network and you can have them say, "I have a need for doing a budget. Do you guys know any line producers?" They're like, "Yeah, here's a man. Here's this company right here." Or you need an editor because you want to put together a sizzle reel or you want to do short film or a teaser for your film or proof of content so people can visually get what it is that you're trying to make.

Or you need a DP [director of photography], where do you find a DP? Well if you're reading Filmmaker Magazine and you're on symposiums and you're on Facebook pages and you're on Twitter and you're on all those places where the filmmakers are, then you can get to the filmmakers and there are hundreds of them. Because if one of them, if five of them are busy, there are three more that may have time to respond to your email, your text, or Facebook post. Do you know what I mean?

SM: As far as distribution strategy, there is so much information out there, and like they say, "People perish for lack of knowledge," most people are not going out to seek for this information. I guess, that's my biggest takeaway so far, content creators have to spend time doing research on how to do these things.

RS: Exactly. That's like saying I want to be a Computer Scientist. Well, you know, the first thing I would recommend if you want to be a computer scientist is

184

you need to spend a lot of time studying and research. You got to learn.

This is no different; it's the same thing in acting. "I want to be an actor. Wait, can you tell me some places I can audition?" Before you audition, have you taken a class? Where did you study to know the craft of what you're doing? Everything in life is all about the craft. If you really want to be good at it, you got to do a lot of research. You have to study, study, and study.

It's different in the classroom. Study means you're studying through the network of people that you built. Do you know what I mean?

SM: What information, regarding distribution, do you find people know the least about?

RS: I feel people don't know anything about distribution. I think most come with a naiveté about distribution. Only distributors they know are usually the ones whose name may have appeared in a film. They might know Sony and the big names but the chances are unless you do an extraordinary film, an indie film with a low budget, it's unlikely that you'll get, or should I say, very few films get that level of distribution.

It's usually going to be smaller distributors like Magnolia. They take on more indie films. But you don't even know how to reach out to them because you don't know they exist.

I feel like there is no one question about distribution that I get other than, and I tell people you can spend the time and learn who, what, when, where, but that's only going to be so helpful because you have to start building relationships with those people ideally.

Because depending on how you bring your films to market – the way often done in the indie film world is, you make a good film; you take it to a festival and try to get a sales rep. Some sales rep will want to rep you because they love your film. The sales rep will then start shopping it around to distributors based on how it did at the festival and the crowd you got at the festival. Then, they sell it to whoever is going to by the film.

That's a relatively passive way for producers to get their work done but it's an accepted way to get stuff done.

185

I have determined that I need to spend more time in understanding more and have direct relationships with distributors so that I can make sure that I leverage the fullest amount of return for my investments. That's a sophisticated thing that I didn't understand having to produce three films over as many years.

That's not something that novice producers in my seminar would ask me. What they would ask me is, "How do I figure out how to get to a distributor?" That's the question that comes up. I'll say, "You can hire a sales rep. They know everybody because that's their job to know everybody." "Well, okay how do I find a sales rep?" "Well, you can find a sales rep in a variety of ways. If you film in a festival, almost every festival I'm involved in has a list of sales rep. They have a list of press people, a list of distributors. They have a list of everybody in the industry to help you to make connects in the industry, to get your film seen somewhere down the line."

SM: What's the key to building these relationships? I'm learning I can't do much without a relationship. It just makes the process so much easier when you have a relationship with people. I also believe in the "big ask." Just ask someone for a soft introduction so that you can get in there and ask the particular questions and start to build a relationship.

But how do you go about building relationships with these people. Is there a key? Is there a way to do it? How do you even get in to say, "Hey can I sit down? I would love to have a chat with you?"

RS: Here's what I do. When I go to film festivals, I walk in a room and I meet with people who I know and I say, "Oh so who's here?" And they say, "That's Ted. He runs so-and-so distribution company. hat's so-and-so. He runs the Indiewire Magazine." And I'll just go and, "Hi I'm Ron. I'm with Simonsays; what do you do?" You literally have to work the room, because you never know who's going to be in the room especially in film festivals, symposiums, or seminars. You don't know who you're talking to. You just have to meet as many people as you possibly can.

You should go out. If you're not giving away at least 25 cards every week to somebody, then you're not serious about networking. If you are in the early stages, and you have no network, you need to be giving away 25 of your business cards and taking 25 business cards a week writing down where you met them, some idea of what they look, put them in your database and when you start doing a newsletter about whatever, keep in contact with them.

It's not about just collating cards. One of the most important things that people overlook is that, "I got the card. I'm connected. I'm good." No, no, no. You have to still have relationships. You have to touch base with them every few weeks. You don't have to always ask them about something. "I wonder if I can ask you about..." Give them something. "I met you. You have a dog and I thought of you when I saw an article on a dog being rescued in Afghanistan."

SM: I learned early on that the key to networking isn't getting something. It's really giving something.

RS: It is giving something. It builds your network so much faster if you give. If your focus is to give, give, give then eventually that person will be a part of your network and when you ask the network, those people who may have a connection with you will respond.

SM: I do have a question about the look book.

The look book is created specifically for investors?

RS: For me it's for the investors, yes.

SM: Cool. What goes into a look book?

RS: There needs to be the director's statement. There needs to be a logline, and a synopsis. There needs to be an idea of what the packaging is, who are the characters. Here are some the actors we're looking at. Here are the actors already cast in the project. Here's what the budget looks like. Here's the genre of the film.

All those things that you would expect to hear in a pitch need to be in there. But it also should give you a sense of the look and feel of the film, the tone, and the color. If I look at this book, I should be able to say, "Oh, I have in my mind an idea of what this is going to

	look like right now because this look book has given me lush pictures of what's going on.
SM:	I'll be transparent with you. I didn't have a look book before. I didn't even know what they were until recently when I talked to someone whose film I acted in last year called *Miles,* with Missy Pile, Paul Reiser, and a few others.
	He was the one who educated me on look books. When I saw his look book, I thought, "Wow! I'm not even in the running for investments without a look book! How can I ever compete with Hollywood! I'm just being really transparent.
RS:	Let me tell you, people will access you based on what you come to them with. Because when people come in and say, "I have nothing but a great idea," I put them in a "this is going to be a ton of work and they clearly don't know anything about the business," category. They don't know anything; they don't understand how many thousands and thousands of projects are out there that are, not just like theirs, but that are head and shoulders above them.
	They have a look book. They have some packaging, an experienced director or an experienced DP or whose screenplay was in the Sundance Screenwriters Lab . I've seen tons of projects that come through because I'm involved in the Sundance Screenwriters Lab .
	So guess what? Whose screenplay am I going to spend more time with? If I had a limited amount of time to read, I'm going to probably read something that Sundance said, "This is a good story." I'm going to probably spend more time on that before I spend it on someone who came in because in his or her point of view, said it's a good project. Because who doesn't think that their project is a good project? That's why would we do our project. Because we believe it's a good project. Other projects will have a seal of approval. The further along you get, the more attractive and easier it will be to get supported. The more money you have.
	If you said to me, "I got two million dollars to make this movie," I can tell you me, and about 20 other

producers in town will go, "Let's sit down and see what you got!"

Or if you told me, "I got no money, but Brad Pitt is going to be the executive producer and I went to the Sundance Screenwriters Lab ," I will be like, "Let me sit down with you. How does Tuesday at 5:00 work?"

Everybody is trying to find the project that is going to move him or her to the next level. That means that I'm working with distributors who are at a certain level and they want to move up to their next level of distributing. They're looking for content that will help them.

You are trying to get on the map are trying to get your project to the next level. That's what the intent is. It's to move the career, the project and your company forward.

So it's about having a real understanding of the competition out there, I think it's a helpful and fruitful thing because that will tell you what you need to do – there's no one baseline but you need to make your project and product as attractive as possible not only to investors but producers because all producers get hundreds and hundreds of submissions every year. The question is why your project is so special and so much better put together and so much further along and so much well-prepared and have so many more experienced people that they want to take time to speak with me.

SM: How do you go about packaging your project? Because you're an executive producer, do your projects primarily come to you packaged by people like a content creator or producer?

RS: Sometimes they do. Sometimes they don't. When I have to package a project, I have a couple of casting directors that I work with so that we can sit down and we go over what will be good for these roles and we go out to make offers. It's either give them an offer because I'm at that stage or give the screenplay into their rep's hands.

SM: First monies. You're trying to get an investor but need the talent to come on board to sell to the investor, or if

	you go after the talent first, they want to know you have money to shoot the project.
RS:	Squeaky, welcome to my world. Welcome to every single project that I do. That is the business that you're walking into.
SM:	It is. And so you just keep pushing.
RS:	You keep pushing. I tell people all the time. What I have to do is I have to create reality out of this clear blue sky. I literally have to create material and substance out of thin air. That means I got to be moving investors into investing at the same time moving talents towards attachment.

Do you know what I'm saying? I'm trying to get everyone. Everyone says, "Let me know when you get, half the money, or all the money or whatever and then I'll consider." The other side is as you said, "Tell me who is in the movie and I'll tell you if I'm willing to invest in it." Which is why you have to start off with, "This is the kind of actor that I want in this role."

SM:	The wish list.
SM:	Exactly. It could be one person. I saw a look book last week. It was amazing. Beautifully rendered, four-colored, multipage, just gorgeous shots. They have Amazon or wherever they're going to shoot it. They haven't gotten any actors attached yet but it gives you a sense of how this is an amazing project even though none of those actors have even been contacted.

They have a beautiful dramatic picture – I can't even remember, Brad Pitt or somebody. It looked really good. What happened is, it emotionally moved me and that's the first step. The first step is to get you excite. That's what a look book is. It doesn't mean there's always a reality there. It just means that this is your vision and you've grabbed them through the beauty. That's what you've done.

SM:	Okay. Well, thank you so much. I appreciate how in-depth you went about what's needed and what's not needed. It will be really helpful.

Jim Arnoff

Packaging Agent, Entertainment Lawyer

Jim was a Television Packaging Agent at the William Morris Agency in New York for 7 years packaging television series, specials and long-form programming for the networks, cable, and syndication. His television projects included *Dr. Ruth*/Lifetime Television Network; *Mother's Day with Joan Lunden*/Lifetime; *Mother's Minutes with Joan Lunden*/ABC; *The Recovery Room* pilot/CBS; *Timeslip* pilot/HBO; *Richard Simmon's Slim Cooking*/first-run syndication; and *Robert Klein Time*/USA Network.

Jim left William Morris to start his own packaging agency. As a packaging agent for reality, non-fiction, documentary, and animation television production companies, Jim works with his clients creating original programming, securing creative/financial elements, arranging for network presentations and negotiating the production/financing agreements. He also works with his clients to secure work-for-hire productions in programming, commercials and on-air ID's/promos. Jim covers the commercial, basic cable, and pay cable networks in New York, LA, Washington (the Discovery Networks) and Atlanta (Cartoon Network/Adult Swim).

He packaged *I FILE* series for first-run syndication and *AMC In Concert at the Rainbow Room* Series/American Movie Classics. He expanded his representation to include animation studios and has packaged *Talking About Sex*/Buzzco Associates, a one-half hour special for Planned Parenthood; *Wake Up America*/Broadway Video/Peter Wallach, a primetime pilot for Fox Network; *Monroe*/The Ink Tank, primetime series development project for FX; *American Girl Magazine*/Buzzco Associates, series development; *Knitwits*/Buzzco Associates/Oxygen; and *The Unpettables*/Curious Pictures for Fox.

Jim's most recent packages include *Nature's Nightmares*/Mechanism Digital primetime series currently in development with The Discovery Channel; *Back Spin*, a one-hour series for Bravo featuring major motion picture actors; *I, Spy* series of 13 ½ hour stop motion episodes produced by The Ink Tank for Scholastic Entertainment/HBO; 12 animated segments produced by B3 Pictures for *Sesame Street*; *Ghetto Simms*, an animated film for *Chappelle's Show*/Comedy Central; and *Will Play Extra* pilot/Lovett Productions/IFC.

In 2006, Jim started packaging original series for the web including over 100 comedy webseries for heavy.com and a pilot for Comedy Central's Motherload. The comedy series for heavy.com include *Burly Sports Comedy Show*, *Smarttec with Ron Jeremy*, *Workout from da Pen* and *From Ashy to Classy* with Donnell Rawlings from *Chappelle's Show*.

For his animation/effects client Mechanism Digital Studios, Jim provides in-programming animation for non-fiction programming, including The History Channel's series, *Engineering an Empire*, The History Channel's movie tie-in specials, *300* and *10,000 BC*, National Geographic Channel's series, *Supermegastructures* and National Geographic Channel's Special, *Inside Grand Central*.

Jim is a faculty member of the School of Visual Arts and teaches "Animation: The Real World" (everything you need to know about animation except how to animate) to senior animation students.
Jim leads workshops, including personal branding, networking, pitching and the art of the deal, for the Producers Guild of America, HBO, National Academy of Television Arts and Sciences, New York Women in Film and Television, The Actors Connection, Women in Children's Media, American Women in Radio and Television, Writers Guild of America, New York Women in Communication, New York Coalition of Professional Women in Arts & Media, Viacom and MTV Networks. He has been a featured speaker on the business and packaging of animation at NYU, Pratt, ASIFA and Women in Animation.

SM: What are some of the biggest mistakes you see happening with content creators with regards to pitching?
JA: One is not creating a relationship first with whomever you are pitching. And that really means that the executive knows who you are. They've got a comfort level. It's also you getting a sense of who they are and where they are coming from so it's a sense of mutuality and respect for each other, rather than just pitching before everyone knows who the other is. So clearly if you've known the executive for a while, or even there, you want to start the pitch out by catching up, "How have you been? What are you doing?" to keep the relationship going and also for them to get a clear sense as to what are you up to. You want to talk very specifically, rather than, "Oh this business is great, I'm doing a lot of different things." hat doesn't mean anything. So, the more specific you are, the

192

more of a connection you make. It's making that strong connection before you pitch. That's number one. Number two is, and this has happened to me and my clients, is pitching something that is so far off the mark for that network's brand that they're thinking, "Do you not watch? Did you not go to the website, know what's coming up?" So really being prepared for, not exactly what they are looking for because they are not always sure, and they rely on you to come up with something they have not seen before. But it has to fit their demo. It has to fit their personality.

Also, bringing in what I call an underdeveloped pitch where you are like, "Okay, that's fine, but where's the hook, where's the excitement, what are you delivering, what makes it special? What's going to make it great to pitch." Because the bar to sell has continually been going up, up, and up. This is why you see all the competition, and different outlets, and platforms. You've got to break through all the clutter and that executive has got to get it. Not only do they have to get the concept, but also here is where the packaging comes in and all of the different elements. The ideal elements are ideally there and they fit beautifully together. It's all of those parts and that's where the packaging comes in.

SM: You've said a lot! The first thing is the "relationship building." How does one go about building relationships? Content creators are always like, "We can't get through the doors."

JA: Well, it's networking. It's building. So, if you don't have a relationship with the network, you are not going to get in. Save the phone call to try to get in to see somebody. That's not how the business works. In fact, that's now how many businesses work. So you build. You use all of your connections to find ideally a production company, or maybe a showrunner, or a senior producer, or editor. You find out what production companies have produced your kind of programming that have been very successful, and then you can start thinking, "How can I get into the door of that company first." "Who might I know?" You do the LinkedIn search. You ask everyone you know, "Hey does anyone know about Phil pictures? Someone might say, "Oh yeah, I know a junior editor over there."

Great. So you meet with the junior editor. And the junior editor might say, "Oh wow, let me have you meet with the senior editor." And then the senior editor might go, "Oh, I know a producer over here." And then the producer may go, "I know someone in development." So it's all a build. You don't have to worry about getting in the door. There is no door, Squeaky. With the right team, there is no door. You go in. It's that simple.

SM: I've say repeatedly to content creators. though I don't think they get it, "You have to ask. Ask people to do soft introductions to help you get in the door? I don't believe that they believe it's just that simple. Everyone knows at least 200 people. They may not all be your best friends and close associates, but we all know at least 200 people. When you do the math, that's about 40,000 people in your network. Somebody has to know somebody in development. So, start asking around.

JA: You have to know what you are asking. You have to be very specific about what you are asking. You can't just say, "Oh, do you know anybody at A&E? I want to get in the door at A&E." If you have no experience, that's a waste of time. You have to do your homework. You have to do your research. Then you say, "Here are the five production companies in New York that fit my programming. These are the five companies I want to get in to see."

SM: I called it the wish list.
JA: I call it the hit list.
SM: I like that. I agree with everything you are saying. I think the biggest problem is that we aren't using our network and asking around. I was speaking in a general sense and will assume that a person will go in knowing about the opportunities they have to offer. Either way, many aren't using their network or asking.

You spoke about elements. What are those elements to packaging?

JA: Well, every project is totally unique unto itself, so it's not just the idea. A lot of folks say, "Oh, I have this fabulous idea and no one has ever done it." That doesn't count. What are you delivering? What asset are you bringing? Is it a talent? Is it access somewhere? Is it a format? Is it a book, a property? What are you bringing that is real intellectual property that no one else can bring? So that even before you start networking or pitching, you have work to do all by yourself. So if you have found a homemaker in Alaska where the dishes are out of control and she has the most charismatic personality, then it's up to you to find her, sign her, shoot her, get a casting reel together. So you have something to pitch. Not, "I have an idea, I'm going to find a fabulous homemaker somewhere that is outrageous and charismatic." That doesn't mean a thing.

SM: When I took your workshop, you talked about the sizzle reel and you mentioned a simple way to create one so that it gets the point across without spending lots of money. Can you talk about that?

JA: Every sizzle will be different. How you shoot it is totally up to you. You really want to have a good team to put it together. First identify if its talent or location, or is it scripted? Are the scripts written? Are you going to shoot a webseries? Or a couple of scenes? Which means casting and location. Or you can simply get actors and put them in a black box theater and shoot that. Something more than just, "I have an idea." You have to come to the position that every idea has been pitched 50 different ways. Right.

SM: For some reason, the show *Dating Naked* comes to mind. I always think, "What was that pitch like? Did they actually go to the island and shoot a sizzle?"

JA: It depends on the strength of the production company. If it's a well-known production company, on occasion, the ideas will sell itself. On occasion with a very strong production company that is known for that kind of programming. So a network could go, "We know your work, you are very successful, you've done this type of programming before, and we are going to trust you on this one. Here is some money, go shoot."

SM: How does an independent content creator partner with a packaging agent?

JA: You have to pitch me the same as a production company or network. It has to be enough there that's going to really impress me and make me say, "Wow, you are delivering something real." There is value in this and I actually want to put my reputation on the line to

195

introduce you to a production company. So you still have to do something on your own first.

SM: So the process is, the content creator or I would pitch you and then you would take the content creator or me to a production company?

JA: Right. Because I represent the companies, I would not represent you. To me, the best package is where the ideal production company is attached, has probably further developed it. They have shot a new sizzle reel, or strike that one, reedited it, added graphics, and really heightened the reel itself. Any network executive, during a pitch, they are looking at everybody in the room. "Is everything I need to know and want in that room?" So the sizzle reel is a strong one, with amazing talent, a format that matches the network's brand, and the ideal production company that they know, respect, and trust is in that room guaranteeing delivery; the creative and financial, then it's more than likely to increase the chances of it moving forward.

SM: You just spoke a heavenly language.

JA: Right. Now that's not to say if somehow an individual has access to a network through his connections, then it's been known that they go in and they pitch and the network says, "Great! Who do you want to attach as a production company?" And then you'd give them your list and the network will say, "Great! Here is our short list. Go meet each one and tell me who you like." That's happened as well. Not as often as you going through a production company, because that's the preferred way to do it.

SM: The production company will help you to further develop your idea and also help you package.

JA: Right, also if you aren't with a production company the network will not give you money or trust you to do anything. That's why they would put you with a production company.

SM: Is there a process or strategy to packaging? If I'm producing a project and wanted to reach out to an agent, would I only go through that agent's talent list? Or do I start from who I want attached?

JA: You'd want to know who is in that particular space in terms of the content, and it's not hard to do that. You see what shows have been on or are on that you respect. They have your kind of sensibility. You look at the end credits to see who's the production company, and EP's [executive producers] are. Then you start to create your wish list, my hit list. Then you go after them.

SM: You have schooled me. Thanks.

Pete Chatmon
Writer and Director

His debut feature, *Premium*, starred Dorian Missick, Zoe Saldana, and Hill Harper and premiered on Showtime after a limited theatrical run. Chatmon also wrote, produced, and directed *761st*, a documentary on the first black tank battalion in WWII, narrated by Andre Braugher. Chatmon received the Tribeca Film Institute "All Access" Program's Creative Promise Narrative Award for the heist screenplay *$FREE.99*, written in collaboration with Candice Sanchez McFarlane. Through Double7 Images, his Digital Studio, he has directed, shot, and edited content for advertising agencies, Porsche, Proctor & Gamble, McDonald's, Universal Pictures, and other brands. Chatmon's career began in 2001 with the Sundance selection of his NYU thesis film, *3D*, starring Kerry Washington. His short film *Black Card* began traveling the international film festival circuit in Spring/Summer 2015 and premiered on HBO in February 2016. Chatmon is also a Sony Pictures Television Diverse Directors Fellow, NBC|Universal Directing Fellow Finalist, Disney|ABC Program Director for the 2016-18 seasons, and HBO Access Directing Fellow where he directed a pilot for the network entitled *Lady Bouncer*. Most recently, he directed *American Koko* for ABC Digital and Viola Davis' JuVee Productions, from a script written by Diarra Oni Kilpatrick. He will be directing an episode in Season 4 of *Black-ish* this Fall.

SM: So you primarily do film?

PC: Well, it's a mixture. I've done features and shorts. I also do a lot of community contacts so stuff for Ad agencies and large and small businesses from Proctor and Gamble to local shops. That's kind of the day in, day out stuff. Now, I'm working on a couple of programs and just got a representation in which I get that first TV episode.

SM: Congrats on getting representation. What was your process in getting representation?

PC: I always use one analogy and it's not that quick, but it's not that long. The thing about what we do as creative people is that it is subjective. That's the distinction, right. If I play basketball and I had 20 points and 10 rebounds, I'm getting drafted there's no doubt about it.

But, if I make a film, it's love or hate. It will be something that you like or don't. There are so many different factors that go into that – power dynamics, race, culture, whoever is behind the desk. It's not like in sports.

The one thing that is the same is you never really get a sports agent to come watch you play. Like in college, you look up in the stand and people say, "Hey that person is from Duke. Or that person is from North Carolina.

With film and the creative arts, I just look at it the same way. I got to keep making as many projects as I can as often as possible, as well as possible in my voice, my level of execution. At some point, maybe somebody will fall in line and like it and get on the train, but I've got to keep the train moving.

The thing that's going to be the end goal is always the level of creative growth and creative expression. After I made *Premium* in 05, we got distribution in 07. In our way, it's $600,000 for this film and I thought certain things would come my way, because I've worked so damn hard to get there but they didn't. I think looking back, the industry was changing. I reached that after my feature as we were beginning to get more into this digital…I'm a writer, director, actor, editor, producer…you know people were kind of just making stuff and sheparding it into the world.

Between that time, I wrote some scripts that I thought people would buy, but they did not. I was growing my production company, doing branded content. In 2014, I just reached out to one of my buddies who had a script that I had read 10 years ago. I asked if he still had it because I got some money from my work for my company, and I wanted to make it work.

So, I made that short film only to really make myself happy to have something to point to that wasn't eight years ago. That film travelled the festival circuit. HBO picked it up. It led to Sony Director's Program. It led me to shadowing on *Silicon Valley* for HBO, shadowing on *Blacklist* for NBC. Then I got all the representation.

But even with representation, they can't do anything unless you're giving stuff to push. So you still have to write, you still have to make short films, you still have to be making content as often as possible, so they have the ability to keep knocking on doors and using their relationships to highlight the work that you do.

SM: First of all, everything you just said was amazing. I like the analogy. I get it. The agents – you don't go ask them to sit in the audience. They come. You find out later on at that moment that you have these particular people and you have to impress. You still have to play hard or on our case have a dynamic script, be willing to shoot the short, go out of our way to find the work, write the work and keep doing it. I get that. That makes a lot of sense.

So, the way you got the representation was coming back eight years later, directing the short, which were official selections in multiple film festivals and reached the agent at the festival?

PC: Right. The irony is, or the joke I have is a $30,000 short did more for me than a $600,000 feature.

SM: Isn't that something?

PC: But then it's like timing. There are all these other factors that come into play. Which is why it always comes down to we just have to make the work for our own happiness. When I finished that film on March 2015, when it was locked picture and I had a video link that I could share with close friends, I was totally satisfied. I have done what I set out to do.

Then when all the things started happening, that's great, but I didn't do it for all those things. I did it so I can look at it and say, "Here's where I stand as a director." I really feel when you look at other folks, and they're just going out there and making and making [films] because they need to, other stuff just comes because the work has a clarity and passion behind it.

SM: Let me ask you, you raised $600,000. How? Was this through crowdfunding or were you out there pitching investors?

PC: We were pitching investors. This was pre-crowdfunding. The first thing, the guiding principle that I have for asking folks for anything is I try and consider, "How would I be in terms of receiving this pitch or presentation?" This goes down to the script, when I write a script and building a character.

I know the first thing the actor is going to do is be like, "Alright, what scene can I get busy in?" So, I got to give you a scene because you're coming to the script like, "Where's it at? Where's it? "Okay, page 50? Okay, yeah, I can rock that.

The investors, what questions are they going to ask? Why are you making this? How do I get my money back? How are you prepared to navigate, explain the landscape of the business of an independent film? What's the worst thing that can happen to me here, you know? And really being prepared to answer all those questions.

What we did was over time you're making a film, I feel like you should present something visual. We had obviously a business plan, and I created an EPK. I made a short film that spoke to the ideas of the feature. And then, we did an investor's presentation and were using that. We did parties and events and anything we could to meet people in New York or Tristate area really aware that you are out here trying to make this film.

As we keep tapping shoulders, people will be able to reach out to whomever they thought will be the person in their network that would know something about that film. That person could say, "I know Pete. I went to that party he throws once a month." Or, "I know Pete. I saw his other short." Do you know what I mean?

SM: So, I'm going to go into an investor meeting differently than I would go into a regular network meeting or pitch meeting. You made an EPK. Some people have look books. You have a business plan. You don't need all of that for a pitch with an actor or a manager of an actor or a network.

What exactly do you bring into an investor meeting?

<table>
<tr><td>PC:</td><td>

I mean there's really no blueprint. I really do think it's all about your story and your style. For me though, for *Premium* in particular the first thing that I made was the electronic press kit. I interviewed all the actors that I have worked with dating back at this point. This was '04 so all the ones I worked with since '98 and had been in my films. I went and interviewed them, asking them questions of how it was working me. And then I intercut clips of films to show how their careers had grown. Like Dorian Missick who was in all my stuff. I'm showing you scenes from my films he was in then a scene with Hugh Grant and Sandra Bullock in *Two Weeks' Notice* at that time and talking about the next film that we're trying to raise money for.

The viewers were looking at it like, "Wow! These people are in the industry. They may be new and fresh but they're putting up the flag now." Then, I interviewed crews as well just to have people say, "This dude has a vision and this project is more than just a film. It's going to be giving a voice to a certain audience that doesn't get an opportunity to be put on camera in a truthful, honest, and realistic way."

Because I wanted to have something creative, I took from the script element and did a short film called, *Confessions of Cool*. The main character's name is Cool. I came up with that idea and put them on a white stage, on a white background, cyc stage. Then, we had them go through all the elements of his character like right through the camera and presented the themes of the film. You could watch that and read the script and not misunderstand what I was trying to do.

Then, we had the business plan like, "Here it is, what we're doing. These are the people on board. These are the people we want to bring on board."

This is how independent film works. Some of the people that you're reaching out to have no idea what to expect. They might get a little blurb in late January about the film that sold $10 million in Sundance, but they don't necessarily know the mechanics of how the industry works. You are kind of explaining how this works and then we're also saying how we're structuring the money. Whatever you're investing in,
</td></tr>
</table>

this is how it breaks down. These are the units and this is how the profit comes back based on whatever deal it's going to be under these percentages.

Then, I guess the fourth thing – the EPK, short, business plan – the fourth thing that we had was the actual investor's agreement with the subscription agreement. That's where it has the legal stuff, who's going to be investing and how much. It actually has all the rules and regulations of the llc to become a silent member and investor in the film.

With those four things, I can go talk to anybody and if it's a great conversation and they're ready to rock, I've got everything that they could need. They can go home and sleep on it. Some folks want to go to the husband or wife. They've got everything they need. They don't have to reinterpret what I've said to them. I've given them everything they need.

SM: Good for you.

PC: The other thing though, you mentioned, you don't necessarily have to do this or that for an actor. In my mind, I think you do. Because there are actors who are making their creative decisions from a business perspective.

SM: Great point.

PC: I think you want to be able to answer every particular angle that someone may have and not make an assumption that, "Well, this is just going to be a creative conversation," because they just do films, because you might find that that person may invest in your joint. You got to be fully prepared to present the totality of your film in a creative and business perspective, in my opinion.

SM: That changes my perspective, actually. Thank you for that.

How do you determine which investors you're going to pitch? Is that huge research? Are you tapping into investors that share the film's point of view because you've done your research or do you say, "Let me reach out to money people."? What's that process like?

PC: It's anybody who's willing to sit down. I think the thing for me is that the idea of the cold call, we're not out here selling Facebook stock. Nobody is really going to be interested, like there's no person dying to throw money at one of the most risky investments that they could ever make. It's like you might as well say, "I'm starting a restaurant."

I think what's important is that you find folks that are either going to know you or have an emotional attachment or investment in what you're trying to do. I think anybody's network is only so large and the best way to expand it is to build your community. There are a variety of ways you can do that.

For me, that was doing the parties that I was throwing because that allowed me to do – just to give you a quick nutshell – what I did, I had an event called The Premium Party and I was charging $10 before midnight, $15 after. It was like a regular party, Saturday night in New York City. At midnight I was going to show a film.

The first party I did, the film was the "EPK", and I don't care. I was trying to get people to come. We got 400 people to come. The next time I went and did this film, I mentioned to you, *Confessions of Cool*. I thought that up and we had Premium Party Part 2 and showed that film the next time. Now, I probably had 600 people who would come to these events.

Now, I have the ability to talk to their network should they come across me in some other environment and say, "Hey, you know this guy. He's trying to raise money for a film." Those elements that I put together and promoted in those parties are what I use in a 50-person investor presentation that I did four or five months later.

SM: Fifty person?

PC: Fifty. Basically from my own network, I said, "who do I know that might have the ability to invest some money?" Some of the people that I've met through all these events and parties and things I've done locally, even in my hometown, doing a short film class in town. I was trying to do anything and everything so that there's a profile of the film, the company, and myself, that doesn't always say, "When you see me coming, I'm going to stop and ask people for money. Because that's what it looks like. It's like these people who email you every week to help their campaign. It's like, what else are you doing when you're not asking me for money?

Putting all those assets together helped us get to a place where we could present the film. Ultimately it was like, maybe only five people I personally knew that I thought might have the ability to contribute. But, along the way, you're asking everybody to refer you to somebody. "Hey, do you know anybody who might venture capitalist?" And they have all the materials that we've already discussed to make it easy for them. They can look at the materials. They can pass them on. Maybe they are like, "Hey this looks alright. Maybe I can give $5,000 and get involved?"

You don't know where those dominoes are going to fall, which is why you just have to cast a wide net and try to find as many folks who can spread the Gospel of Squeaky, right? [Laughter] Get it to as many people as possible. Somewhere along the line it will click.

SM: So, distribution. *Premium*, you had a distribution deal two years later. How did you go about getting it? Are there any tips that you can give?

PC: It's funny because sometimes the simplest thing is what it is. You know like somebody asks you for advice and what you tell them sounds like a cliché, that's as true as can be. But it isn't like, "Do this first…"

I just believe if you make films that are just good, honest, and well-executed, that's your responsibility. Beyond that, at this level, you can try and say, "If I put this person in it, then I'll get distribution." I've seen plenty of films with recognizable people not get distribution.

Sometimes you're weighing these decisions, and in no way will I say, if you have to choose between a named actor and some no-name actor, I'm going to say go with the named actor. There are things that you can overthink. I think it comes down to making sure that the film is well-written, the voice is clear, and you know what you're working for.

205

	Then, the chips fall where they may. I think we have to go into these projects without distribution, because I don't know if I even want them to exist.
SM:	Yeah, absolutely.
PC:	I'm not saying they don't want them to exist. Sometimes they don't get it. I have this film that got picked up by HBO. It's called *Black Card*.
SM:	I saw it.
PC:	I have another script that I'm pushing in and even my reps are saying "no"… I just want to make a point right now. All the comments you're saying, you would have had the same comments on the script with *Black Card*. Some stuff you just don't get. You need to see it for it to translate.
SM:	Yeah, when I was watching *Black Card*, "I had that okay, I see where this is going," moment. If I were reading the script, especially the first couple of pages I would think, "Where is this headed?" I agree it's subjective. I mean so many great works get passed over. It's very subjective. It all depends on how much time they have, who read it, what they're in to, all of that. I totally get that. I really liked *Black Card*.
PC:	I kind strayed from the question. As far as distribution, how we got it. I'll give you the full circle. How do we best sell this project to find support both from the investors, to the crew, to the cast and from audience and building a community? Then, how do we make everything on set? How do we make the best decisions to take what we set out to do in pre-production and protect it? Then, it's made, and we go and run the Festival circuit and promote the hell out of the film, still trying to use our network to try to get as many people to come and see it, to get emails in front of folks who are decision makers. Then, we just kind of hope it connects with the audience and the right people to see it and want to pick it up. We had our deal with *Code Black*. They saw the film at Miami International and in a couple other film festivals and saw the reaction was good and kind of sprung from that. Today, if you don't get a distribution deal, you have so many self-distribution channels that are incredible

	avenues to make revenue, but you got to work it yourself.
SM:	Self -distribution channels... like?
PC:	Like you can do Vimeo and charge people with their tip jar or pay-per-view or you can do VHX. VHX.TV is a great site that shows that indie film, *Indie Game the movie*; they turned down a distribution deal. It's a documentary about independent video game makers which is very similar to us as filmmakers. They turned the deal down and turned to VHX. They are selling that joint at $14.99 per download.
SM:	Technically Amazon or Create Spaces as well, you can do your video through them.
PC:	You keep all that dough. It wouldn't be like "Oh we spent $20,000 on your website and we got to recoup this." Do you know what I mean? And you don't need to have millions of people to see it. You may have 100,000 people see it and you can make more than you would if a million people see it.
SM:	Because it's 100% yours.
PC:	Right.
SM:	*Premium* was presented in the film festival circuit, and after seeing it quite a few times at different festivals they offered a deal?
PC:	Yes.
SM:	So, with *Black Card*, that was at ABFF [American Black Film Festival?
PC:	That was at ABFF.
SM:	How do you pitch to your actors? Like Dorian Missick?
PC:	With *Black Card*, that was me making phone calls. Everybody in there I knew, like Dorian suggested his wife. And I talked to his wife and was like, "Yeah, let's talk make it happen." To be quite honest, you really have to make the best decisions for your project. Like I initially, I was thinking, I want to get Nicole Behari. I kind of know her. But to be honest, we up here shooting in my apartment and I've got people here sitting on the couch, getting their make-up done, until they have to leave the room because somebody has to change their clothes. It's not the way it's supposed to be and I know somebody like that

	[Simone Missick] is going to be perfect in understanding what we're doing here.
SM:	Understanding the movement rather than, "I'm in Hollywood. This is what I'm used to. You got to make it right for me."
PC:	But for something like *Premium*, the feature. It started with Dorian. You're locking in people that you know. I was talking to as many people as I know as possible because again, those are folks that you can get on board. I had begun in the beginning talking to Mike Ealy. I actually had Kerry Washington attached because she had done my short film at NYU and Sundance and that fell through.
	Once we got the money, it was like, you're casting a director and you're talking about who's ideal for the project and who will actually respond to it.
SM:	Your wish list.
PC:	It ain't like you out here thinking, "Let's get Meryl Streep," when you know she would never do any of it. You kind of figure out who the right people are.
SM:	So you eventually got a casting director rather than doing it yourself.
PC:	Yeah, if you've got 35-40 roles to fill and some of them are just a day, some are cameo; it starts to get far beyond your relationships.
SM:	And time. That alone is enough to get a casting director, to save time.
	Pete, those are all the questions I have. I'm so happy that you were able to talk to me and help me help others. I really appreciate it.
PC:	Thank you.

Gary Lico
Global Distribution of Forensic Files

Gary is a 40-year veteran of TV program sales, development, production, research, scheduling, and even hosted a TV talk-show! For more than 20 years, Gary Lico ran the company he founded, CABLEready; the first programming company dedicated exclusively to US cable networks.

Original programs developed by Gary over the years include *Forensic Files®, Inside the Actors Studio, Monster Quest, Deals From The Darkside, Intersections, Saw Dogs, Women Behind Bars* and scores of others. CABLEready's third party, global representation business partnered with rights holders like Discovery, National Geographic, Reelz, TruTV, TV Guide and top independent producers such as Medstar Television, LMNO, Hoff Productions, Burrud Films and many more.

SM: You helped develop *Forensic Files*, can you tell me what was the experience of pitching it like?

GL: Those were the old days, Squeaky. When a little company like me, I was really almost one guy at that point, can represent a little company of Pennsylvania and take an idea into a cable network. I was known, but the production company was not known. This was the time when I had a much better chance of selling a show. In this particular case it was born pretty simply by me as a consultant going into Allentown, Pennsylvania where these guys are located – Netstar television is the name of the company. They hired me to come in for a day and come up with some things they could do. It was around the time of the OJ trial and these guys were doing medical programming. I said to them, "Look you are doing this medical stuff – what they were doing was this medical insert, you know when you're watching the news and they say, "Here is the latest in foot fungus?" They would do the foot fungus footage – On the OJ thing I said, listen of all of your medical reporting, do you happen to know Dr. Henry Lee, who was you may recall one of the witnesses for the defense. So they said, "Oh yeah we know him. He was at the time, the most well-known forensic scientist in the business, a business that was growing at that point.

So, I came up with the title, *Medical Detective* and a show that would basically take one case every episode and dissect it from a forensic point of view where science catches the bad guy. So he did a 5-minute teaser video that I pitched around and they said, "we will give it a shot," and we got the money to produce one episode and it did it great. I did a scene, with the buyer from TLC at a convention over in Europe that I go to two times a year, and he said, "It did great, we're giving it a series order" and with that it took off. I was suddenly in the international sales business, because the producer was able to keep all right. So as a result, there was great opportunity. It was 20 years ago, Squeaky.

SM: So when a show is pick up internationally, the producer keeps the rights?

GL: No, not much today. In fact, I was talking with one of the Discovery Networks yesterday and she said, "We prefer to own all the rights." That is because there are so many mergers and acquisitions. What was once one little network might be Scripps network now. What was once a little Discovery network is now a huge company. They want to own all the stuff they telecast. There are some times when you can keep the rights. Foreign producers are able to do much better because the laws are stricter. But, in the US if you are going to produce something, be ready to be a producer for hire. In fact, there is a big court case going on right now about this a lawsuit from Discovery and a production company as to who owns footage if Discovery cancels the show.

SM: I have a format show that I created and I was talking with an executive producer and her thoughts were to start pitching it internationally first.

GL: It depends on if there is some sort of international appeal to it. I will say that some networks will buy a program based on a paper format but only if there is a production company involved in it.

SM: Many content creators are clueless of the process of distribution and how it works.

GL: No kidding.

SM: So could you speak to me about the process of getting distribution?

GL: The process is you would talk to an agent or to a production company, which is the best bet. Let's say you have a program about outdoor action; real, non-fiction, outdoor action, okay? Well then you ask yourself, "Who does programming like that?" Ok, well it is Original Productions, "Who do I talk to there that would be producing something like this? Who would I talk to there about my idea?" That is really what it amounts to, that is your step. From there what you are going to do is try to hold on to it as much as you can to be a producer. Because they can walk into a discovery and say, "Hey, this idea came to us, we can be the Godfather on this; we can be the guardian angel." And they will in essence, they or your agent will become your representatives. Then someone within their company is going to handle distribution. They might have a deal with a company to handle all of the distribution – any program that comes through the front door. In a nutshell that is kind of it. Now of course the networks are going to get their mitts on it. And they are going to want to have their cake on your idea. They are going to make notes on it and second-guess you on probably, most everything, because you are a first-time producer. You are not Ron Howard. You are not going to walk in there and say, "This is my vision." No, your vision is right now a part of our vision. [Laughter] So, you better catch up with it.

SM: How do you hold on to your vision?

GL: It is very difficult for a new person, it just is. How do you hold on to it? Not on your first deal. You become easy to work with the first go around and then you'll get another shot. I have producers that were only doing one program and they never really connected with the network. So they were very expendable. The show was good, but it wasn't that unique. The network was going in a different direction. They could have renewed it, because this guy was a rookie and he didn't have anything to lose by saying "no." It wasn't like he wasn't going to come to them on their next show.

SM: I would like to talk further talk about connecting with the network. You have the middleman, who is the production company, and then you as the producer/creator of the show, how does one maintain that connection with the network so that they are known through the process and they are able to build that relationship?

GL: You will. How do you do it? In that case you just do it. I haven't always been good about that. When a show is in production, I kind of let the producers handle things. I think maybe in some cases I should have been closer and checking on them every few months.

SM: So, the production company is responsible for getting the show distributed. As a producer, what should we NOT do when it comes to negotiating?

GL: As a first-time producer?

SM: Yes.

GL: The best way is not to care if you lose the negotiation. If you go in saying, "I don't give a darn if I don't get this deal. That gives you a power. The equally best way is to have a good attorney in that business looking out for your interest. It should be an entertainment lawyer because it gets very complicated.

GL: I would recommend taking a look at a book called, *Stop or I'll Shoot*.

SM: What is about?

GL: It's about a show on TV, but is a pretty good walk-through about a lot of what we've been talking about. She does a weekly newsletter on the programs that have been picked up and that sort of thing.

SM: Well, I just wanted to ask you a few questions, as I said before, there are so many who are clueless to the world of distribution.

GL: That is the only way some programs make money. They are in a deficit in the US and make up their money around the world. It is also controlled by big companies, whether it's Comcast, Disney, Time Warner, Viacom, Fox, CBS. Internationally, BBC, Sky, Discovery [to name a few]. They want to own everything and in doing so they will distribute everything. A lot of times when they have their meetings, the sales and distribution side will meet with the programmers as well, and say, "Yeah, that will be popular around the world or people are looking for that we shouldn't do another show like that." International is that important; if it is not, "Have a good day," you know.

SM: I really appreciate you taking time out of your day.

GL: Oh no problem. And don't overwork yourself you need your health. If you have any follow up let me know.

J. Alexander Martin

Co-Founder of FUBU, President of FUBU TV

J. Alexander Martin headed an empire built by originality, urban influence and industry changing music.

The acclaimed **J. Alexander Martin** has externalized many successful ventures in the fashion industry including the iconic clothing line FUBU –"For Us By Us" – serving as the co-founder and Vice President. Today, his kingdom includes a clothing line, a non-profit and a consulting firm. Through all of his endeavors, it is his innate talent and ability to predict trends that has caused him to impact the world once again. J is the CEO of FUBU Television (For Us By Us), with broadcast agreements with Dish Network, Verizon Fios, Xfinity Comcast and Frontier. FUBU TV is also available digitally on iOS, Android, FilmOn, Apple Tv Roku and the Web. FUBU Television Network features multi cultural/urban lifestyle related programming. FUBU-TV.com - Worldwide Reach 250 million

SM: J., there are so many people who just don't know how to pitch their idea. I've made a lot of mistakes myself. Which is why I've set out to share my journey and seek the answers from people who have bridged the gap. That's what this interview will be about.

JM: I would like to tackle the start, if I may. And I'm probably going to go on a tangent. Can I go?

SM: Yes. [Laughter]

JM: The problem in life, and the problem with advice and with people is the first start. Because all of the people want to start where people ended. Most people look to see what somebody else did and say, "Well, they got this done" or they got done, at the point of you know with us, of a million dollar sales. They never look at day one.

SM: They never consider all you had to do to get there…

JM: Not only all it took to get there, but the start. The "Okay, I'm going to sacrifice my days – partition my days – into putting food on the table and trying to create something." And most people can't get that right. They always want to start in the middle.

SM: I totally agree with what you are saying about how

214

people look at the end result of a person's success, and don't see the grind, hard work, the bad days, and failing so you can get back up and start the cycle again. And it's a huge mistake we may have all made.

Based on the mistakes you've made in the past, what advice could you give on pitching?

JM: The first thing of pitching an idea is pitching it to yourself. And second, there is a problem with that, because the average person thinks whatever their thing is, is the best thing since slice bread. So, the second step is to get out your own way.

SM: How do you propose we do that?

JM: This is the thing, you go off and you propose your idea to as many people that you know will give you the best feedback. You want them to tell you it's not going to work. People get all upset about a hater, "Oh he's a hater." No! He or she is not a hater. She gave you feedback to show you that this could happen so you can go in a different direction. I never start a business until I've gone through every reason why it won't work. And once I finish this exercise of going through the cons, then it works. Why? Because I've done the homework. The problem is everyone wants a dollar and a dream, but the problem is most people don't want to get up in the morning to go get the lottery ticket.

Another thing you need is a partner. Why? Because what you can't do, your partner can. Sometimes when you are trying to pitch your words may get jumbled up. So you need someone who can articulate your ideas in a certain fashion that someone will say, "Yes, I want to invest my time or money."

Thirdly, no one is here to finance your dreams. So if you don't put any money, time, and sweat equity into it, why should they? Alright, I'm sorry. I'm done. [Laughter]

SM: Let's talk about the sweat equity. So, if someone comes to you, and they've done the work creating and are seeking an investor, what do you say to them?

JM I don't want to hear it. No one wants to hear it. My job when you come to me is for me to get everything I can out of you, and the best for me. So when you come to me, your idea switches. See people have to think of it that way. You have to work it so that people come to you.

215

You have to let the people know that you are willing and able to accept their proposal. That's how you have to think about it. It's not about you going to them and saying I need money. That rarely ever works. It's about them saying to you, "I need to give you money, so I can make more money." That's what the investors have to come and say. Whatever you have to do to make that happen is what you have to do. I mean that's another chapter, but that's the formula, compared to, "Investor, can you please give me money?"

SM: I like that. I guess Issa Rae would be a great example of that? Right?

JM: Yeah, that's one example. I'm speaking of someone who writes a script, creates a trailer or sizzle, and starts running around looking for money because they want to create this great big project. Sometimes, it's not a matter of turning it into a bigger project. I think a lot of times what people do throws a monkey wrench into your pitch and your life because it brings negativity into the situation. A businessperson that you pitch may say, "I already have something like that," and they want something else. So you walk away feeling down without ever looking at what you accomplished. But if you could look at what you accomplish first...writing a great script, take that and turn it into something more. Like I said, the best way you can get money is somebody coming to give it to you. You always have to look back at what you accomplished. Someone may look and say, "Oh, I'm *only* on a digital platform." What do you mean, "only?" You did great! Now continue doing great. But don't give up to go try to find someone to be your savior because now your 100% turns into 15%, 25%, 45%...You have to take what you have, and keep building on your success. The first success is just starting it, your second success is continuing it until no one can deny you and someone wants to come in and help. I know a lot of people who will take a movie that they've already created and turn it into webisodes. Webisodes are garnering more attention than movies, sitcoms, series – or as much.

SM: So you are saying don't create a short film, then start to look for someone else to see your dreams through, keep doing what you are doing?

JM: Think of ways to continue what you are doing in that same ability. Do what's in your capacity and people never do, because people go from a and look at z and say, "I want to be there." Don't think like that. I understand that's your goal to be there, but you can't run the philosophy of building a business that way because you will always fail, unless you get lucky from doing it a different way. But 9 times out of 10 it's not going to happen that way.

SM: Well, certainly people are buying into other people's dreams, you take *Birth of a Nation* for instance...

JM: That was an anomaly. That doesn't happen every day. It was the right time; the right message.
Another thing people don't do. They don't do their homework. They don't research, don't look, or you don't follow. You may follow social media, but follow and look to see what people are doing. There is a whole world that is telling on the internet what's going on, but you're still thinking, "I got a better idea." The proof is right there telling you want it wants. People are telling you want they want. You have to know how to follow and create trends. Those people [like Nate Parker] happen to have the right product, at the right time with the right quality, and it was good enough. Just like FUBU, when we started it was the right time, right everything.

SM: Any tips on actually pitching?

JM: Yeah, business is not all about numbers. It's about the person. That's half the battle. It's about the personalities of the people involved.

SM: Well, J. "Having people come to you," is such a great perspective and piece of advice. I'm so thankful that you made the time for me to interview you.

JM: Yeah, sure.

CONCLUSION

I've learned many lessons about pitching while on my journey to pitch 100 times, most of which I've taught you in this book. Where I am today, versus a year ago, is almost like the difference between night and day. The strategies I've given to you, I use every single day.

Several of my biggest lessons, however, probably have little to do with the act of pitching itself and more about life, and I would be remiss not to share those with you too. Lessons from a success mindset and how to identify failure, or the importance of staying the course are all a few of the valuable lessons I've learned while on my journey.

One of my biggest lessons centers on overcoming the feelings of rejection and is at the top of the list of lessons learned. On this journey, I realized that there were so many reasons why my show ideas hadn't gone all the way to series. Some things were beyond my control, and the timing just wasn't right, and some lessons I needed to know and improve upon. Among them all, here are the most important life lessons I've learned:

"No is not universal." This came to me as a huge revelation one day while listening to Pat Flynn's podcast, *Smart Passive Income,* with guest, Jiao Jiang. Jiang spoke about the rejection he felt after pitching and how it paralyzed him and made him feel like he needed to go back to the job he'd left to follow his dreams. Jiang taught me to change from being reactive to proactive in my pitching process and in life. He taught me to make a conscious decision of what I can control and to distinguish quickly the things I can't control. It's a waste of time to cry over what I can't control, but I could live and intentionally make things happen that I could control. This is what brought me to pitch 100 times. I *could* control becoming the best pitcher possible!

Saying "no" to myself is worse than being told "no" by someone else. This is one of the best lessons to learn in life! Have you ever taken yourself out of the running before someone else did? Decided you weren't good enough to do this or that? That was me. On this journey, I learned some valuable lessons around self-worth and valuing self. I realized that most of the time, I had an inner-dialogue that would talk me right out of greatness. This scene would play out in my head:
Me: Squeaky you should do this to be great. Start now to put the things in place to be great. Step out now.

Inner voice: Are you sure you can do that? What makes you the expert or authority on this? Surely, there are people more qualified than you to do that! What will people think? But you've never done this, that, or the other before, how can you do that?

Me: Maybe I shouldn't. I'll wait until I get a few more whatevers before stepping out to do that.

Sound familiar? Well, Donald Trump's presidential campaign is the best way I can justify the point I am making. Many of us will look at a list of qualifications and because we are shy two or three of the entire list of qualifications, we decide we aren't right for the job, or that we shouldn't be seated at the table. But Donald Trump, with almost no political experience, never quit, never seemed to doubt his capabilities, or allowed people to talk him down from presidency. He stood completely convinced he was right for the job! He was sure that what he didn't know, he could figure it out. His presidential win changed my thinking around valuing self, self-worth, and "qualifications." I made a decision not to take myself out of any race anymore! I learned to completely trust my skills and myself, and what I don't know is simply an ask or book or try away.

I learned how little I esteemed my creativity and myself during this process. Donald Trump is just one example of this, but there are many filmmakers and TV show creators who simply took a stab at it and are succeeding! They didn't have any prior training. They had passion and ambition, and that is what won!

I retrained my mind to believe that I am supposed to be at the table with other talented content creators, no matter how many successful shows or films they have and no matter how few I have. My ideas are brilliant. Period. I was rejecting myself by taking myself out of the race. Because I was told "not now" didn't mean I wasn't worthy enough to be at the table. It certainly didn't mean that I wasn't creative enough. Jia Jiang said, "Rejection and acceptance is about that person. You can give the same presentation to different people and will get a different answer." It was a lesson for me to pitch my ideas to everyone and every company that is right with a belief that they should want my idea because it was the one that would bring them millions of dollars. Now, at the top of each day, I ask myself:

Squeaky, what would you do today if you knew you were the best at what you did?

Development. The shows and pitches I created weren't the only thing in development. On my journey to pitch 100 times, *I* went into development too. In the past, I would spend much time on developing my skill as an actress, writer, producer, or director, but I never put energy into developing other key areas like in business, marketing, branding, goal setting, strategic planning, and selling. Limiting my development to creativity was hurting me in a big way. As an independent content creator, we have to develop ourselves on many levels because we don't have the conglomerates, their numerous departments, executives, and big budgets to help us see our projects through to fruition. If we are to succeed as content creators, we have to be very strategic in our planning and actions across the board. It doesn't help us to be amazing writers and directors but be ignorant about the business or how to market or brand our projects and ourselves. Likewise, it can hurt us if we are great at all of those things but are too afraid to step past our fears to actually market the project. If we create an amazing project, but do not believe in our capabilities enough to pitch it to network or studios, then it doesn't matter. If rejection can stop us from going all the way with our dreams, then we've failed ourselves developmentally. There were so many areas that needed strengthening if I was going to succeed. My journey helped grow my faith, taught me to value myself, taught me to promote myself even when I didn't feel worthy of the promotion; it taught me to ask big and take bold steps. It taught me how to self-motivate when I was uninspired, all of which is needed in an industry where you hear "no" more often than "yes."

In order to grow as a whole, I had to do some soul searching and be very honest with myself about where I stood. It was a humbling experience, but one well worth it. Now, when goal-setting at the beginning of each year, I make sure I've included a well-rounded list of development goals in areas that will stretch me creatively, spiritually, emotionally, intuitively, and in my business mindset.

The importance of gaining visibility. As independent content creators, our daily goal is or should be about gaining visibility. In order to get ahead of marketing this book, getting in front of development executives, investors, and talent, and growing my audience, I had to learn how to toot my own horn. Becoming visible to people in high places is a skill. Becoming visible to my target audience took a lot of work. I had to be bold, act confidently, and value myself, and what I have said tremendously to bring attention to myself, my work, and potentially be judged.

I became a thought-leader during this journey by trusting my knowledge and taking the risk to put myself on display while telling people the strategies in which to pitch. To put myself out there to be observed, and judged, and potentially putting yourself on the chopping block to be called out as "having it all wrong" is pretty scary. What I am doing, the secrets I have told and giving step-by-step strategies, I don't believe has been done before, at least not in the way I am doing it. I took a risk at being wrong! But, I believe many doors have opened and are opening because I have spent the better part of two years sharing my journey and giving away my pitching lessons. I believe as I continue to put myself out there (on social media), people began to take notice. It is part of the reason I believe I was invited in the room to pitch WE TV. In this digital age, we should be using the Internet to help us achieve infinite possibilities and visibility.

Break Some Rules. Throughout my journey, I found myself constantly preaching to content creators I coached or ones who attended my workshops against discouragement of "getting through the doors." A message I repeated often is "I've been able to walk through them without having representation," My motto has always been to "think outside of the box," or "ask big in order to walk through the door. I believe so few people walk through them because so few actually try to." It was on a pitching call with the Head of Television of Sales for Centric TV and BET Soul, Michelle Thornton that the light bulb went off. (I met her at our son's AAU basketball games and later asked for a meeting after seeing her at an entertainment event).

We were wrapping up our meeting when she was telling me to follow up with her on a TV idea that came to mind during our call and to feel free to call her on her cell. I respectfully said, "Are you sure? I want to make sure I respect your time," I don't want to go against the rules." And she said something profound, at least to the people who are in the business of trying to break through or break in. She said, "Girl, in order to be great and get the things we want, we are going to have to break some rules." Boom. That message resonated with me for days following our call. It is where I stand today. It's my new mantra and on the top of the list of rules I now follow on my new journey, #BreakingtheRules: 100 Rules to Break in Order to Break Into The Business.

221

I hope this book taught you a lot about the business of pitching and even about the entertainment business. Like I said in the beginning, if you were able to walk away with one piece of information that could help catapult your career to its next level, then my job here is done and I am winning!

Until we meet again, create continuously, pitch perfectly, and break some rules!

ABOUT THE AUTHOR

"One woman, many faces, one creator many talents," is how Squeaky Moore likes to describe herself. As a writer, director and producer, Squeaky's mission is to enlighten, uplift, and inspire. Squeaky's career path – one designed to artistically address socially conscious issues and invoke discussion for the greater good – lies at the very core of who she is and is continually reflected in her work.

A Chicago native, Squeaky received an MFA from Roosevelt University's Conservatory. A natural storyteller with a "gift for gab," she began using her gifts in 1999 after she created and staged a variety show "Ack Like U know", which served as catalyst to her starting her production company, Moore Squeaky Productions.
She later created an improv-based comedy show "Guud Timez based on the 1970's," *Good Times* TV sitcom, followed by staging *The Ugly Man.*

Squeaky moved to New York City to pursue acting but would soon transition into fulfilling her true passion for writing, directing and producing after *64*, a project on father-absent homes that she produced and assistant directed, became a viral sensation. *Your Black World* described it as "Life changing and powerful." On the heels of *64*, Squeaky produced, *Father's Day?* a film that addresses the effects of absentee fathers, which debuted on the launch of Magic Johnson's Aspire TV Network. Some of Squeaky's recent directing and producing credits include *The Positive Controversy*, a show in which she developed and is the show-runner, and her latest film project, *Face of Darkness - Journey to Healing*, a documentary film that explores depression and suicide in the African-American communities.

Squeaky has been featured in *Huffington Post*, Centric-TV, *Madamenoire, Bossip, The Examiner, News One, Amsterdam News,* and forecasted as a "woman to watch," in *Ambition Magazine* for her work as producer, director and writer. Visit her personal website at www.squeakymoore.com

Made in the USA
Middletown, DE
20 August 2017